LET'S TALK TURKEY (ABOUT JAPANESE TURKEYS)

and OTHER TALES from
THE ASIAN WALL STREET JOURNAL

D1422243

LET'S TALK TURKEY (ABOUT JAPANESE TURKEYS)

and OTHER TALES from THE ASIAN WALL STREET JOURNAL

edited by Urban C. Lehner

CHARLES E. TUTTLE COMPANY
Rutland , Vermont & Tokyo, Japan

Visit Tuttle Web on the Internet at:
http://www.tuttle.co.jp/~tuttle/

Published by the Charles E. Tuttle Company, Inc.
of Rutland, Vermont & Tokyo, Japan
with editorial offices at 2-6 Suido 1-chome, Bunkyo-ku, Tokyo 112

© 1996 Dow Jones Publishing Company (Asia) Inc.

LCC Card No. 95-61323
ISBN 0-8048-2051-1

First edition, 1996

Printed in Japan

TABLE OF CONTENTS

INTRODUCTION

No otherwise serious newspaper revels in the quirky like the global Wall Street Journal. The Journal's three papers—The Wall Street Journal, The Asian Wall Street Journal and The Wall Street Journal Europe—are renowned for running one offbeat story on the front page every day. Written to entertain as much as to enlighten, these stories touch on everything from the sex life of the sea cucumber to the comeback of the barbershop shave—anything but the bread-and-butter business and financial stories that are the paper's normal grist.

The Journal and Japan were made for each other, then, because few countries harbor more quirky stories waiting to be told. There is an indefinable something about the Japanese, individually and collectively, that makes them fascinating to foreigners even when (or perhaps especially when) they're trying hard not to reveal much of themselves. Whatever the reason for the fascination, Japan over the years has proved enormously fertile ground for those offbeat front-page Journal pieces, known to insiders as "a-heds." (The name derives from the "a-hed" headline style used on the stories in some Journal editions, which coincidentally resembles a letter A.)

This book is a collection of some of the best a-heds on Japan that have graced the front pages of The Asian Wall Street Journal. It is, thus, a look at the lighter, more human side of Japan. An introduction to fascinating characters like the Pink Lady and the Egg King. A glimpse at the peculiarly

Japanese ingenuity that brought the world such curiosities as "capsule Inns" and hole-in-one insurance. An investigation of the psyche of a nation whose television game shows include a competition by a panel of sushi eaters to see who can stand the most green wasabi horseradish.

The stories are reprinted as they appeared in The Asian Wall Street Journal; many of them also appeared in The Wall Street Journal, although sometimes in slightly different form. The two papers share a common majority owner, New York-based Dow Jones & Co., a common eight-reporter Tokyo bureau and a common right to run each other's copy. They are, however, separate newspapers, separately edited for very different readerships.

The Wall Street Journal, founded in 1882, has a circulation of 1.8 million, almost all in North America. The WSJ posted its first correspondent to Tokyo in the 1930s.

The Asian Wall Street Journal, which celebrated its 20th anniversary September 1, 1996, posted its first correspondent to Tokyo soon after it began publication in 1976. Headquartered in Hong Kong and printed in Hong Kong, Tokyo, Singapore, Kuala Lumpur and Bangkok, the AWSJ is a 51,000-circulation, five-day-a-week newspaper that covers Asian business the way The Wall Street Journal covers American business. It has a staff of 60 reporters and editors in 15 Asian cities writing Asian news and features for a readership that is 70% Asian. It also offers superior coverage of American and European business from its sister Journals overseas.

For 12 of the past 16 years, it has been my honor to play a role in the writing and editing of many of these stories during two tours as Tokyo bureau chief and since 1992 as editor-in-chief of The Asian Wall Street Journal. In the editing of this volume, I have received invaluable advice and research assistance from Hiroko Fujita and Miho Inada, the Journal's able news assistants in Tokyo, from Dolly Wong, the AWSJ's librarian in Hong Kong, and from Michael Williams, formerly a reporter in the Journal's Tokyo bureau. Judy Chan and Eveline Phu in Hong Kong did much of the tedious work of preparing the manuscript. My thanks to them, and also to the other people who made the book possible—authors of the a-heds themselves.

The stories chosen for this book represent only a small proportion of the a-heds on Japan the AWSJ has printed, and inevitably some good ones have had to be omitted. I have tried to pick those that best grapple with the question I think most interests foreigners: Who are the Japanese, anyway, and what makes them tick, after all?

— URBAN C. LEHNER

SECTION ONE

TRADITION AND CHANGE

大里四

Introduction

The more things change, the more they stay the same. A Frenchman takes credit for that piquant truism, but a Japanese could have authored it just as easily. For few societies have experienced as much superficial change and as little fundamental change as Japan.

Consider the Japanese bath. On the surface, much has changed. The old public-bath houses, the *sento*, are dying out; most newer Japanese homes come equipped with tubs. But the important thing, the distinctive Japanese way of bathing, hasn't changed much at all. The tub is still a place for leisurely soaking; the washing is still done outside the tub, and the soap is still carefully rinsed off before entering it. The same steaming bath water is still often used by several bathers, either simultaneously or successively.

Or consider relationships between the sexes. On the surface, again, much has changed. Younger Japanese women are much better educated than their mothers, and recent changes in Japanese laws enable women with university degrees to have real careers. They are no longer limited to working as tea ladies. And yet the important thing, the structures and rhythms of Japanese relationships, haven't changed much at all. Many educated women still willingly give up their careers when they marry to devote themselves to husband and children. Most still accept that they will see little of their husbands at nights and on weekends. Although arranged marriages are less common than they once were and love matches more common than in the past, marriage is still as much about one's obligations to parents and society as it is about meeting Mr. or Ms. Right. So is staying married: Divorce is still rare, and still greatly frowned on.

Contrast this underlying constancy with the dizzying change in family relationships in some Western countries. In the U.S., for example, the proportion of children born out of wedlock went from 5% in 1960 to 30% in 1992. In France, it went from 6% in 1960 to 33% in 1992. In Japan, it was 1% in 1960, and 1% in 1992. Unchanged.

Perhaps Japan will experience more real change in the future than it has in the past. But if the stories in this section have any common underlying theme, it's that we should be wary of simplistic assumptions about the nature, or pace, of that change. Sometimes when Westerners inquire whether Japan is changing, they are really wondering whether it is becoming more like the West. The answer is yes and no. The changes are not all in one direction. The final outcome is unpredictable.

And while Japan can turn on a dime when a crisis requires it, most of the time change comes to the Japanese as John Steinbeck said it comes to most human beings: like a little wind that ruffles the curtains at dawn, like the stealthy perfume of wildflowers hidden in the grass.

* * *

Old Japanese Inns Attract Status-Conscious Foreigners

> *EDITOR'S NOTE: First-time visitors are often disappointed that modern-day Japan doesn't look or feel more "Japanese." The visitor is looking for something more like the Japan depicted in 19th-century woodblock prints. He wants his women in kimono and his men in yukata. He wants arched stone bridges over lily ponds leading to charming pagodas. He wants, in other words, the Japan that today is available only at a place like Tawaraya.*

KYOTO—An ancient bellhop in Oriental pajamas. A woman in kimono, on her hands and knees, bowing to guests as they arrive. A hallway lighted by a giant candle. A guest room with sliding doors, a lantern, an antique hanging scroll and a private garden.

Tawaraya is both lodge and landmark. It is small, just 19 rooms. It is old, dating back to the early 1700s. And it may be the most tradition-minded inn in this most tradition-minded of all Japanese cities. One of the most expensive, too. One night for two people can easily add up to $500.

> *"Here in this simple room, there was no noise. With the beauty and simplicity, you really felt it was a spiritual moment."*

Tawaraya isn't just expensive; it has snob appeal. Kyoto may boast 1,500 Buddhist temples and 200 Shinto shrines, but when it comes to status symbols, the holy of holies may be right here.

References Required
The people who run Tawaraya certainly cultivate an aura of exclusivity. House rules say new customers must be recommended by previous ones. "This is a very special style of inn," says Toshi Sato, the middle-aged proprietress whose family has run the inn for 11 generations. "Most of the time we need an introduction."

Some Japanese travel agents refuse to phone the place for reservations. Even the Japan National Tourist Organization, which gladly helps visitors book rooms in any other Kyoto inn, won't touch Tawaraya. "If somebody comes in and wants to stay at Tawaraya, we just tell these tourists, 'Here is the phone number. You can call,'" says Toru Ohkata, the manager of the organization's Kyoto office.

Over the centuries, many ordinary Japanese have passed muster, but the inn's owners seem to cherish most the princes, business barons, political leaders and famous novelists who have spent the night. Over the past several decades, Tawaraya has attracted a great many famous foreigners, too.

The inn's guest books attest to some of the larger American and European egos. Alfred Hitchcock and Peter Ustinov left self-portraits in them. Leonard Bernstein and Stephen Sondheim left bits of hand-scrawled music. Jean-Paul Sartre signed his name in Japanese characters. Paul Samuelson, the Nobel economist, set forth an intricate economic formula, then explained in a footnote, "An eternal truth for an eternally serene place."

Mrs. Sato's "eternally serene place" has become so busy with the foreign-tourist trade that she has established a quota. Only 40% of the rooms are allocated to non-Japanese. "Otherwise we would fill the inn with 100% foreign guests, since foreigners make reservations further in advance," Mrs. Sato says. Valued Japanese customers could never get in.

Tourism officials discern a trend. More and more Americans and Europeans want the "authentic" Japanese experience when they visit Kyoto, so they stay in a Japanese-style inn, *ryokan,* sleep on futons and eat Japanese food. Meanwhile, Japanese tourists in Japan show an increasing preference for Western hotels. For one thing, although Japan is one of the safest countries in the world, some Japanese say they like the security of rooms with locks and keys, which are lacking in authentic old Japanese inns.

Charge for Prestige
"Western hotels are more comfortable and less expensive,"

says Fumitake Yoshida, professor emeritus of chemical engineering at Kyoto University. He recoils at the thought of putting up friends at the most expensive Japanese-style inns. "They charge mostly for prestige," he says.

Business is strong at the top of the line, though. The consensus is that three Kyoto inns are in the highest class—Tawaraya, Hiiragiya and Sumiya. The first two are across the street from each other. Hiiragiya is somewhat larger, with 39 rooms, and is less austere than Tawaraya. They are friendly rivals across the pavement, constituting a sort of Harvard and Yale of Japanese inns: Some people are impressed if you have been there.

An overnight stay at one of these three inns can be an education in Japanese hospitality. Soon after a guest's arrival, the chambermaid brings tea. Later the guest takes a bath; the water has already been drawn, to 40 degrees Celsius for Japanese guests, about 37 degrees for foreigners. At 6 p.m. or so, the chambermaid arrives with dinner, a multitude of small courses.

The food is one reason the bill is so high. Breakfast and dinner are usually included, and an elaborate dinner often accounts for more than $100 of the charges. Many diners, therefore, expect perfection.

Tough Tuna

Edward Guiliano of New York City is mildly disappointed. Sitting in the tearoom of Hiiragiya inn, he says the raw fish at dinner the previous night didn't match the sushi at his favorite place in Greenwich Village. "The sushi here with dinner wasn't first-class," says Mr. Guiliano, a professor of English at New York Institute of Technology. "The *maguro* (tuna) was too tough. It should be like butter."

His wife, Mireille, however, is impressed by the atmosphere of the inn. "I'm a vice president of a champagne company, and I've visited some of the most luxurious hotels in the world," she says. "But here in this simple room, there was no noise. With the beauty and simplicity, you really felt it was a spiritual moment."

The best ryokans spare little expense in pampering their guests. They serve the food on top-quality lacquerware. They keep extensive dossiers listing their customers' favorite dishes, favorite types of pillows and favorite chambermaids. Hiiragiya has a staff of almost 60 for 39 rooms. Tawaraya has 38 full-timers for 19 rooms, including six people who do nothing but gardening and cleaning out the hot tubs. It replaces the cedar tubs every five years, at a cost of about $20,000. Every 10 years the bathroom paneling of Chinese black pine is replaced because it loses its fragrance.

Clearly there is a clientele for this. There are also travelers who wouldn't dream of staying in such a place. "A complete waste of money," says an American banker in Tokyo.

More and more American and European travelers in Japan are turning to cut-rate ryokans instead. One of the most popular no-frills Japanese inns in Kyoto is Hiraiwa. It offers clean, private rooms for $18 a person, and the rooms have been adapted for foreign tourists, with coin laundries, doors with locks and keys, and television sets that give you a choice of Japanese or English audio when you are watching one of the few programs broadcast in both languages.

At a time when many Japanese have stopped staying at the cheaper Japanese-style inns, and many such inns have gone out of business, Hiraiwa has been going great guns. "Last year we had 9,000 guests," says proprietor Saburo Hiraiwa, although this year business is off a bit because of the steep appreciation of the yen.

Fewer Stars
Hiraiwa can't claim the same traffic in international stars as

its more exclusive counterparts. But it has its share of discerning partisans. James Cahill, a professor of art history at the University of California at Berkeley and one of the world's leading authorities on Oriental art, is fond of the place. So are officials of various foreign embassies in Tokyo.

There are a few differences, of course, between what $250 a night and $18 a night will bring.

At Tawaraya, everybody has a private bath and private outdoor garden. No such luck at Hiraiwa. The bathroom is shared. There isn't any garden. There are no chambermaids to spread the futon bedding at night; you do it yourself. And the meals aren't served in the rooms but in the kitchen, where Mr. and Mrs. Hiraiwa themselves eat.

A standard breakfast is $1.20, a bit extra for eggs or bacon. It's just like home. Well, almost. A sign over the kitchen table states: "Please pay before we serve you."

— BERNARD WYSOCKI JR.

September 12, 1986

* * *

Japan's Artisan Skills Facing Extinction

EDITOR'S NOTE: The death of a craft, any craft, is an occasion for mourning. Few of us these days require the services of a blacksmith or a cooper, yet we fervently wish at least a few of them could survive to pass their specialized know-how down to future generations. In Japan, the government has tried to preserve the country's few remaining combmakers, swordsmiths, puppeteers and others by naming a certain number of them "living national treasures." Even so, it's clear that many of Japan's artisanal traditions are in their final generation.

TOKYO—Ask Kiyoshi Kato his profession, and he will pull out a gleaming steel sword with a wooden handle. Mr. Kato, a swordsmith like his father and grandfather before him, will explain how he takes a jagged lump of raw metal and, using techniques more than 1,000 years old, turns it into a weapon fit for a samurai.

But if you ask Mr. Kato how he pays his bills, he will carefully put the sword aside and nod toward a front room of his house. There, he and his wife have a small store selling paint, wrenches, scissors and pliers. It is a little demeaning for a swordsmith to sell hardware, especially since it is the kind of industrial product that is driving craftsmen out of business. But Mr. Kato has no choice.

"It is very difficult today to make a living just from swords," he says. "There are some people who do that, but I think their lives must be very hard."

Art and Lost Art

One of the remarkable things about Japan is its ability, more than 100 years after its industrial revolution, to support swordsmiths, combmakers, puppeteers, *Kabuki* actors and others who work much as craftsmen did for centuries in feudal Japan.

One by one, however, such people are disappearing, and the secrets handed down to them for generations are being lost. Mr. Kato, for instance, has no son, and the apprentices he has taken in over the years all have quit in frustration.

Chances are good that in another 20 or 30 years, his line, too, will come to an end.

"Young people aren't much interested in traditional crafts anymore," says a foreign-ministry official. "Most of the products are too expensive for ordinary people to own, and few really understand them anyhow."

Craftsmen find it hard to change old ways. Mitsumasa Minekawa, the sixth in a line of master combmakers that goes back 300 years, has been carving combs for 40 years. A visitor to Mr. Minekawa's shop is likely to get advice on his hair whether he asks for it or not.

> *"My father was known as the god of combs. Today, no one uses our combs anymore."*

"Try this," Mr. Minekawa tells a visitor, proffering a polished wooden comb with tiny, closely spaced teeth. The visitor's hair is thinning, and Mr. Minekawa thinks he can help.

Scalp Will Tingle

"The teeth will comb each hair individually," the combmaker explains. "The wood is flexible, so the comb won't pull your hair or tear it. It will actually make your scalp tingle."

Sure enough, the boxwood comb, carved more than a decade ago by Mr. Minekawa's father, does make the scalp tingle. Mr. Minekawa grins knowingly. "Prime Minister Nakasone has one just like it," he says. The comb should last at least 80 years, Mr. Minekawa says, until the teeth wear away completely.

But if you want to get your own 80-year comb, you had

better hurry. Fewer and fewer Japanese women are wearing the elaborate hairdos that once kept Mr. Minekawa's ancestors busy, and Mr. Minekawa, who is 63, thinks he will be the last of his family to carve combs. His masterpieces cost $100 and more, and there is little demand for them. "My father was known as the god of combs," says Mr. Minekawa, his eyes glistening. "Today, no one uses our combs anymore."

Some parts of Mr. Minekawa's craft already are dead. Many of the combs, such as the one with the tiny teeth for balding men, were carved by Mr. Minekawa's father, who died working, at the age of 85. The son says that no one, not even he, knows how to do that delicate work today.

Because the boxwood for his combs must dry for as long as 50 years, Mr. Minekawa carves combs from wood his father and grandfather laid away. If future generations are to follow, he needs to buy and store wood for them. But business is so slack, he says, that he no longer bothers. "I have enough left for 10 or 20 years," he says. "After that, I don't know what will happen."

One of the biggest problems in traditional arts is that learning may take decades. Apprentices these days often give up in despair. In *Bunraku*, Japanese puppeteering, the puppeteers themselves appear on stage beside their puppets, and their elaborate movements can take a lifetime to learn.

Years of Legwork

The new puppeteer spends his first seven years studying only the puppet's legs. If he does well, he is allowed to devote his next seven years to the left hand. Only then does he graduate to the head and the right hand, which are manipulated together, and which he is expected to study 10 years more.

"To play the head in a very important role you must study 40 to 50 years," says Rodayu Toyotake V (known professionally as Rodayu V), a Bunraku singer whose songs narrate the performances. Learning to narrate, he adds, can be harder still, since the narrator must learn 150 different styles of singing, none of them written down.

In exchange for his diligence, the puppeteering apprentice is paid only about $240 a month. With government stipends and special pay for touring with the performers, he can hope to earn about $5,000 a year. Rodayu says that apprentices often live for years in tiny rooms whose only plumbing is a single water basin, until they become prominent performers. He himself moonlights as a Kabuki singer to make ends meet. The most talented young people, he adds, no longer even apply.

"To survive in Bunraku today, you must be without any interest in money or desire for goods," says Rodayu. "Unfortunately, many young people today think they should be compensated for their work. I think so, too."

Even Kabuki, the best-known Japanese theater, has trouble recruiting actors. Both Kabuki and Bunraku now are obliged to obtain young performers through government-sponsored schools. But Rodayu complains that the schools don't train as well as the traditional apprenticeship, and he says graduates rarely become leading performers.

By sponsoring schools and granting subsidies, the Japanese government is trying to prevent crafts from disappearing. One of the government's most publicized efforts was the creation in 1955 of the title "living national treasure," which is conferred on at most 35 artisans and 35 theater people at any one time. In addition to a $9,000 yearly government stipend, living national treasures can hope to see the prices of their products go up fivefold or tenfold.

Aspiring National Treasures

Some craftsmen, including swordsmiths, hang on in large part in hope of becoming national treasures. Others, such as potters, have managed to maintain broad popularity by selling their wares in department stores as household art, and to students of flower arranging or the traditional tea ceremony. Aspiring national treasures bide their time making sake cups and flower pots, as well as decorative bowls that look remarkably like ashtrays and sell for hundreds of dollars apiece.

Mr. Kato, the swordsmith, is making his own kind of painful adjustments. He compares his craft to preparing a pie crust, one difference being that each sword takes him a month to complete. He heats the metal and then carefully flattens and folds it over and over, a process that hardens the steel and forces out impurities. Sometimes, after a month's work, he is dissatisfied, so he melts the sword down and starts again. Now 41 years old, he has on average made fewer than three swords a year in the past 21 years since his father began teaching him the craft.

Mr. Kato's problem is that after World War II Japan hasn't needed many swords. To make ends meet, Mr. Kato's father was obliged years ago to begin making knives, work that a purist swordsmith considers humiliating. At first, he made collectors' knives and woodcarving knives with elaborate handles. But today, the family also makes fish-slicing and vegetable-carving knives, so carefully turned out and so expensive that usually only professional cooks buy them. And then there is the Katos' hardware business.

"The best thing for a swordsmith is just making the swords, not the selling," explains Mr. Kato, who in his worn green shirt looks a bit like an auto mechanic. "The trouble is, you can't live like that. I feel very lonely because so few people buy swords. But it can't be helped—it's the flow of the times."

— E.S. BROWNING

August 14, 1986

Japanese Firms Offer Eternal Corporate Togetherness

EDITOR'S NOTE: No doubt about it, the Japanese revere their dead. More: They talk to their deceased ancestors. A young Japanese who is contemplating marriage or a relocation overseas thinks nothing of going to the cemetery to explain the situation to grandfather. The custom both bestows a form of immortality on the ancestor and maintains the connectedness of generation to generation. Even some Japanese companies get in on the act.

OSAKA—One gray day last December, the president of Asahi Breweries Co. secretly gave hundreds of employees the lowdown on the company's results. But none of them rushed to call their brokers.

Where they are, they don't need brokers.

Like tens of thousands of other loyal—and deceased—workers in Japan, 673 Asahi employees have been enshrined at a company memorial after their deaths. Their bodies have long since been disposed of by their families. But on the rice-paper pages of a barley-colored book, their names, job titles, tenures and dates of death are meticulously kept by the company. About twice a year, Asahi's senior executives show up at the black-marble shrine to install new names and appease their late colleagues' souls with detailed reports on the company's progress.

"The workers spend more than half their lives at the company, and we should return their commitment," says Naoki Izumiya, an Asahi spokesman. "One of the unique Japanese characteristics is a common consciousness. We want to preserve it."

> *"To be enshrined gives a feeling of relief to Japanese workers. Their spirits can be together always."*

And so, as if the lifelong workplace traditions of exercising together each morning, laboring and drinking together into the night and playing golf together on weekends weren't enough, more and more Japanese employees are being offered eternal corporate togetherness. In most cases, that means having your name included on a permanent record attached to a stone monument.

"It may look unusual to Americans that people belonging to different religions and backgrounds are enshrined in the same monument," says a spokesman for Ezaki Glico Co., a candy company that has memorialized 88 employees at its corporate temple. "But to be enshrined gives a feeling of relief to Japanese workers. Their spirits can be together always."

Employees seem to like the idea. A quick survey of a few dozen workers at Asahi's main brewery in Osaka shows that five out of six employees are happy to spend forever with their co-workers. Some aim at nothing less than posterity. "I want to leave a footnote showing that I existed in this company," says Kimito Kawamura, a 28-year-old Asahi-brewery worker.

Of course, a few younger employees aren't quite ready to be enshrined. "I don't think I have contributed enough to the company," a 23-year-old woman politely demurs.

Management experts say company shrines foster loyalty at Japanese companies. Malcolm Salter, a professor at Harvard University's graduate business school, visited Asahi's shrine and says the sentiments it fosters aren't phony. The practice of "honoring and remembering employees," he says, "is part of the ongoing renewal of the company."

Companies with memorials say they don't really expect employees' attitudes to change just because their employer keeps a shrine to workers. "We aren't expecting employees to appreciate the company for this," says Eiro Hamada, a personnel manager at Kubota Corp., a diversified industrial group that has kept a shrine since 1952. "Our way of thinking is simply to tie what employees of the past have done to what employees today are doing. It is very Japanese."

Actually, it is very Kansai, the ancient region around Osaka. Companies in Tokyo and elsewhere in Japan sometimes help the families of deceased employees in crowded urban areas to arrange burial plots. But few have company shrines. "What's that?" asks a spokesman for a big Tokyo bank, when informed some companies have shrines. "Does it cost money?"

Yes, they do. The Asahi shrine, which is two years old, cost more than $3 million. But some cost as much as $5 million, and services can run to $100,000 each year. Indeed that may be one reason that it is mainly companies with strong earnings, such as Asahi, that are splurging on splashy, new shrines.

Unlike Asahi, most tradition-bound Japanese companies in this area keep their memorials at Koyasan, a 1,000-year-old Buddhist mission 850 meters above sea level in the lush, steep mountains outside Osaka.

Nowadays, a stroll among the graceful stone memorials is like a walk through an industrial park. There, under the towering Japanese cedars, Matsushita Electric Industrial Co. remembers thousands of its deceased employees in a rough-hewn granite temple. Embossed on a polished, black-marble slab is a testament to hundreds of Sharp Corp.'s late workers. A cast-bronze statue of two uniformed workers marks Nissan Motor Co.'s memorial.

What sets the corporate memorials apart from the older, more traditional temples hidden away in the woods is their expansive, sometimes lavish, design.

Most peculiarly Japanese of all, however, are the squat stone or wood boxes that signal the entrance to each company shrine. They are for depositing *meishi,* business cards. "Companies with business relationships will put their meishi in to show that they are thinking of their old business connections," says Taiei Gotoh, a dark-robed, 31-year-old Buddhist priest whose hair is shorter than his eyelashes.

Just as business is business, industrial competitors don't let ceremony stand in the way of rivalry, either. "Matsushita's memorial may be bigger than ours," says Kubota's Mr. Hamada, unprovoked. "But the value of a memorial isn't decided by size but by mind."

With such fierce emotions on display, the local priest, Mr. Gotoh, is not only an authority on company shrines but is knowledgeable on the recent history of Japanese industry, too. He knows how companies are doing and whom they are at war with because he attends the sort of company updates that Asahi's president delivered to the spirits of his late employees.

Before and after the semiannual pilgrimages that executives make to their company shrines, the official visitors and relatives of the deceased gather in the priest's gilt-edged, incense-tinged temple for remembrance of employees who died in the previous year. Names are entered in ink in the company's memorial books and onto computer lists to ensure that personnel departments remember each year to send out condolences on the anniversaries of employees' deaths.

For Mr. Gotoh, this year's September service for Matsushita will mark a significant milestone in the tradition of company memorials, for along with 300 employees of the company, the group's renowned founder, Konosuke Matsushita, will be enshrined. Mr. Matsushita, who died last May, was the "god of Japanese management," Mr. Gotoh says. It was he who founded the idea of company memorials when he converted his family shrine into a company temple in 1938.

And his employees are still grateful. "For people like us, to be employed at Matsushita means to put our whole life into that company," says Teruo Karasawa, a general manager at Matsushita. "With a shrine, the feeling of belonging lasts forever."

— MARCUS W. BRAUCHLI

August 8, 1989

* * *

Japanese Rituals Show Private Doubts About Abortion

EDITOR'S NOTE: Edwin Reischauer once noted that in Japan, "there is little condemnation of sexual acts but only anxiety over their social consequences." The anxiety reaches a crescendo when the consequences include abortion, which has been widely practiced in Japan since the end of World War II. Since this story appeared, the number of abortions has declined as indicated in the accompanying chart. But the birth-control pill is still illegal.

TOKYO—Tucked away in a quiet corner on the grounds of the vast Zojoji temple here stretch rows of small stone figures. Many hold bright, multicolored pinwheels, blades rotating briskly in the breeze. Others are dressed in stocking caps or bibs. Lying at their feet are flowers, chocolate bars, baby bottles full of milk, dolls, kites and even letters.

One note found near a statue reads: "Tsubasachan, I'm sorry I couldn't give birth to you. I would have loved to put my arms around you even once. . . . Please go to heaven and live happily there." It is signed "Your Mother."

Japanese women, and sometimes men, erect the statues, called Jizos, for a simple but powerful reason: to atone for abortions. It is, says Toshiko Seto, a gynecologist and one of Japan's 11,892 licensed abortionists, "a way of saying sorry to the fetus."

Rising Controversy

In Japan, as in the U.S., abortion excites a lot of conflicting feelings these days. A budding political movement to tighten the country's abortion laws has stirred debate between religious and feminist groups, with arguments similar to those of American "right-to-lifers" and "pro-choice" advocates. There also is rising dismay over the incidence of abortion among Japanese teenagers.

Nevertheless, compared with the U.S., public controversy over abortion here is fairly new and far less heated. Concerns are still more profoundly expressed on a personal level, and underscoring the difference are the extraordinary rituals to which Japanese turn to convey their own mixed emotions.

Many people here are in a position to have such feelings. In 1947, fearing the effects of a new population boom on this already cramped country, the Japanese government liberalized its laws to allow abortion for economic reasons. The change, in effect, made abortion available on demand, and in the 10 years that followed, the country's birth rate fell drastically, from 34 to 17 births a year for every 1,000 people. Abortion suddenly became one of the most accepted forms of birth control in Japan.

> *One note found near a statue erected to help atone for guilt reads: "Tsubasachan, I'm sorry I couldn't give birth to you. . . . Please go to heaven and live happily there." It is signed "Your Mother."*

Today, modern birth-control methods are more widely available (the pill, though, is still banned for fear of side effects), and the number of abortions has been gradually falling. Still, 596,569 were reported in 1981. Says Mitsue Yamada, an official of a Japanese feminist group, "One out of every three women walking down the street between the ages of 25 and 40 has had an abortion."

Experts say the typical Japanese woman who has an abortion is the one next door: married, two children, someone who uses birth control, though this time unsuccessfully. Even so, an abortion isn't something the woman next door likes to admit to her neighbors.

In Takase on the island of Shikoku, most of the visitors to a Buddhist temple that offers services for aborted fetuses come from out of town so they won't be seen by acquaintances. Likewise, according to Seikyo Morita, a monk at the temple, when women in Takase have abortions, they go to religious services elsewhere.

Many Japanese women who have had abortions say they feel guilty or ashamed; some who have had them years earlier report recurring bad dreams. In the view of Soho Tagaya, a monk at the Zojoji temple, their feelings are prompted less by philosophical or religious considerations than a purely emotional response.

In some countries, the moral debate over abortion revolves around the question of when a fetus becomes a human being—at the moment of conception or some later point. But the Japanese don't engage in such fine distinctions. Mr. Tagaya, for instance, argues that regardless of when the fetus becomes human, it is a "life" from the moment of conception and taking "life" is wrong.

Historic Differences

Some also connect the rising sense of concern over abortions with Japan's increased prosperity. Historians note that in previous centuries it wasn't uncommon for Japanese living in rural areas to rid themselves of babies they couldn't feed by killing them. Likewise, in the poverty of the immediate post-World-War-II era, many Japanese honestly felt they had economic reasons for having abortions. Guilt, or at least the ritualistic expression of it in things like Jizos, the infant statues, was rare.

"It's economics," says Dr. Seto, the abortionist. "When we were poor, we didn't have the space in our hearts to build Jizos. We had to survive."

But as their wealth grew, Japanese found themselves with more space in their hearts for guilt and shame. And for something else: fright. For all their fascination with modern technology, many Japanese are superstitious. Some who have had abortions fear that the spirit of the fetus will come back to take its revenge unless appeased, monks say. Others begin coming to the temple 20 or 30 years after abortions when

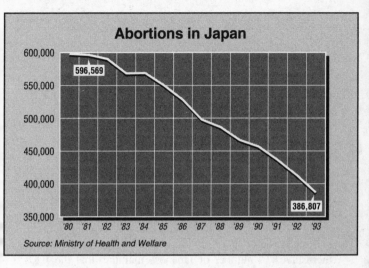

Abortions in Japan

596,569

386,807

'80 '81 '82 '83 '84 '85 '86 '87 '88 '89 '90 '91 '92 '93

Source: Ministry of Health and Welfare

they start having medical problems that doctors can't seem to cure.

"One woman in her 50s confessed she had 16 abortions when she was young," says Mr. Morita, the monk in Takase.

Starting in the late 1950s, Buddhist temples throughout Japan began offering special services in which men and women can atone for their guilt over abortions. Typically, the service involves prayers, perhaps a homily by the monk, the lighting of incense, sometimes the erection of Jizos. A number of services also promise to exorcise vengeful spirits.

Partly because poverty has become much less of a problem in Japan, some people here would prefer to see the country's laws tightened to eliminate abortions for economic reasons. A new religious group called Seicho-no-ie argues that abortions should be permitted only on a strict case-by-case basis when some form of hardship is involved. Feminist groups, however, have launched a counterattack, asserting that abortion should be a matter of individual choice.

The rising number of abortions among teenagers, meanwhile, is seen by some Japanese as evidence of incipient moral decay. Last year, according to government figures, women aged 15 to 19 accounted for 5.5% of the abortions in Japan, up sharply from previous years. The popular press frequently reports stories about teenagers taking up collections among their friends to raise the equivalent of $415 needed for an abortion.

'Like Christmas Cake'

Some blame the problem on the import of "free-sex" notions from the U.S. Others point the finger at television. "Today kids see nude bodies and people sleeping together in their living rooms," says Mr. Tagaya, the monk at the Zojoji temple.

Finally, there is a growing controversy over the rituals themselves. A number of Japanese maintain that the Jizos and other practices are simply a money-raising gambit promoted by the temples. Mr. Morita, whose temple in Takase charges the equivalent of $115 to perform the service, concedes that may be partly true, but he blames the producers of the stone statues rather than the temples for pushing the trend. "Like Christmas cake [a popular treat in Japan that has no equivalent in the U.S.]," he says, "this was started by merchants."

Yet to many Japanese, none of that seems to matter much. And Dr. Seto, the abortionist in Tokyo, contends the rituals still fill a need. Their rising popularity, she says, results from people "feeling bad about killing their babies."

— URBAN C. LEHNER

January 10, 1983

* * *

Etiquette at Japan's Biggest Bank Bows to Equality

EDITOR'S NOTE: Does Japan ever change? Japanologists debate the question endlessly. The believers in change point to the latest generation of twentysomething Japanese and remark on how different they are from their parents. The doubters retort that every generation seems different when they're in their 20s, only to become just like their parents by the time they're 35. The doubters add that it's the workplace that does the final job of molding young Japanese along traditional Japanese lines. But what if the workplace itself starts to change?

TOKYO—Will Japanese corporate etiquette ever be the same?

Dai-Ichi Kangyo Bank, the world's largest, has ordered its employees to stop the practice of addressing each other differently depending on rank.

In most Japanese organizations, a subordinate wouldn't dream of calling his boss Tanaka-san or Watanabe-san, which is how most Japanese address each other in everyday life. Most Japanese companies and government agencies indoctrinate their employees in hierarchical forms of address that in the West are confined to the military.

Thus, when a subordinate addresses a senior in Japan, he says *kacho* for section chief or *bucho* for department head; if he uses the senior's name it's always with the title, as in Tanaka-kacho. Similarly, subordinates are always addressed by name plus a suffix that indicates they are of lower rank or age, like Tanaka-kun.

But now Dai-Ichi Kangyo is trying to change all that. Since

April 1, all of the bank's employees are supposed to address each other the same way regardless of age, rank or sex—last name, plus *san,* the Japanese equivalent of Mr., Miss or Mrs.

The idea is "to promote open and free communication."

The idea is "to promote open and free communication" within the bank, says Akiyoshi Shoji, the bucho in charge of public relations, who is now just plain Shoji-san to his colleagues.

The change is part of a new campaign to make the bank more responsive to customer needs, Mr. Shoji continues. Dai-Ichi Kangyo knows that lower-ranking employees are in closer contact with customers and more likely to reflect the "voices of the customers" in their thinking. But when a subordinate has to address a senior deferentially at a meeting, he is less likely to express his opinion frankly, Mr. Shoji explains.

A trickling of other companies, including Sony Corp., Kao Corp. and Shiseido Co., already practice *san-zuke,* as the usage of the san suffix is called. But banks are among the most conservative of Japanese organizations, and Dai-Ichi Kangyo is one of the most conservative banks. Bank of Tokyo, which has a tradition of being more international and less traditional, is apparently the only other major bank to eschew hierarchical forms of address.

Dai-Ichi Kangyo's new *kaicho,* chairman, Kunji Miyazaki, waxes eloquent about the change. "We're getting rid of the class system. We're treating people equally. We're imitating America," he says.

But for employees of long standing, the change is going to take some getting used to. "I would hesitate to call the chairman Miyazaki-san," says one senior manager. Responds

Mr. Miyazaki: "We know we're going to have to work at this. I'm going to have to keep telling people, 'Please don't call me chairman.'"

Companies that already practice san-zuke say it not only encourages communication but discourages the extreme title-consciousness and obsession with the organization chart that's typical in Japanese companies. If you missed the announcement that a particular *jomu*, managing director, was elevated to *senmu*, senior managing director, you don't risk committing a gaffe.

But it also takes some of the fun out of being promoted. Says a recently appointed Dai-Ichi Kangyo bucho: "Some of my fellow buchos think it's not fair. We just got named bucho, and we'd like to be called bucho for a while."

— URBAN C. LEHNER

April 20, 1992

* * *

Japan Plays Fast and Loose With Definition of Work

EDITOR'S NOTE: People overseas see Japanese as workaholic drones. Japanese see themselves the same way. But as any foreigner who has ever worked in a Japanese office will testify, it isn't as simple as that. Yes, the Japanese put in long hours at the office. But how do they spend those hours, exactly, anyway? When Japanese politicians started blaming U.S. trade deficits on an eroding American work ethic, it seemed like a good time to seek answers to that question.

TOKYO—Let us stipulate right away that most Japanese people work hard. Whether or not the country's politicians have a realistic view of the American work ethic, none dare call the Japanese lazy.

So there has to be another explanation for the scene at the New Shimbashi building here, a garish stucco-and-metal structure crammed with video-game arcades, mah-jongg parlors and bookstores. At 3 p.m. on an overcast winter day, many of these amusement emporiums are crowded to capacity with white-collar "salarymen."

> *"Didn't some economist say it's better if you take a couple of hours of rest in the middle of the day?"*

For some reason, they don't seem eager to discuss laziness in America with an inquiring reporter. "Uh, I just dropped in to see what the others are doing," says a middle-aged man carrying a briefcase, bolting from a second-floor video-game shop. Another middle-aged man in a suit, asked if he has a job, barks "No!" and beats a retreat.

Up on the fourth floor, 50 men in business dress sit at 25 tables playing the board game Go, while several others stand in the doorways watching the action or waiting their turn. One onlooker, a 55-year-old auto-parts salesman, says he often visits Go parlors between appointments. "Wasn't it Keynes or some American economist who said it's better for efficiency if you take a couple of hours of rest in the middle of the day instead of working for eight or nine hours straight?" he asks. On the chance that his boss may feel differently about efficiency, he declines to give his name.

The average Japanese worker spends 2,100 hours on the

job a year, compared with only 1,900 for the average American and 1,500 for the average German. But some Japanese people clearly don't spend all 2,100 of those hours working. If they did, Japan's bankruptcy courts would be littered with the wreckage of pachinko parlors and other businesses that depend heavily on the patronage of truants. Even when they are in the office, some white-collar Japanese workers seem to spend an inordinate amount of time reading newspapers or chatting with friends.

Fiddling around during working hours is a venerable tradition in Japan. A Tokyo woman who worked as a newscaster in the early 1970s recalls that her station kept a blackboard listing which journalists weren't at their desks and why. The reasons included *shuzai,* reporting, and *shucho,* a business trip, but the most popular designation, she says, was *uchiawase,* a conveniently vague word that literally means an appointment but is broad enough to cover anything from running an errand to taking in a movie.

Japanese people work because they have to, or out of a sense of loyalty to their company. In a poll conducted last year by the Chubu Productivity Center, 11% of the Japanese respondents said they would rather not work, a preference shared by only 4% of the American respondents.

In Japan, people work long hours when they have a crash project to finish, or because they need the overtime pay, or because of social pressure. They hesitate to leave when others, particularly the boss, are staying late. Their work and family culture is built around the idea that men return home late, but they can't afford to go drinking with colleagues every night, so they hang around the office until all hours.

Some also complain that they are trapped in a vicious circle: Because they put in such long hours, they can't work flat out all day long, but because they don't work flat out, they need to put in long hours. "If we stopped loafing and worked seriously during the day, we could leave at closing time," declares Yasuhiro Kobayashi, an editorial writer for the Asahi Shimbun, who confesses to sneaking out to a coffee shop on occasion.

Eager to promote daytime trade, some businesses appeal to the mixture of self-pity and pride that many Japanese feel about their hard work. "Rest for overworked you," reads an advertisement for the New Central Hotel in Tokyo's Kanda district, which offers "daytime service" from 10 a.m. to 4 p.m. The hotel rents single rooms for two hours for the equivalent of $17.69, double rooms for about twice that amount. Takeru Takahashi, the hotel's manager, says that during the annual high-school baseball tournament in August, some businessmen steal away from work and rent rooms to watch the games on television.

Despite the "you deserve it" advertising, many Japanese truants don't seriously attempt to justify their behavior. Rather, they look at it as the equivalent of crossing against a red light, something they feel they can get away with if everyone else is doing it.

In Japanese factories, needless to say, there are many fewer opportunities for slacking off. A Japanese factory worker rarely finds himself with a second between tasks to catch his breath; the time-study engineers usually find the second first.

But fields such as sales and financial services have managed to keep the time-study engineers at bay. Standing outside a video-game arcade in the New Shimbashi building, Yuji Hayakawa, a 25-year-old stockbroker, says he has a quota to meet and when he meets it, he often retreats to a coffee shop to read. So are Americans lazy? "I have never seen an American stockbroker working, but my impression is that we play around more than they do," Mr. Hayakawa says.

Recently, articles about frittering away time have started to pop up in the Japanese press. The Yomiuri Shimbun, Japan's

largest daily paper, even coined a term for it: *yukyu sabori,*
getting paid for truancy.

These articles have a long way to go, however, before they
catch up with the spate of stories about *karoshi.* That means
death from overwork.

— URBAN C. LEHNER

March 2, 1992

*   *   *

Introduction

Traditionalists bemoan the homogenizing effects of modernization, and with good reason. Can a newly developing country both enjoy rapid economic growth and preserve its unique cultural heritage? The example of Japan is in some ways not encouraging.

Modern, urban Japan has swallowed American fast-food culture whole. Modern, urban Japan has lost many of those distinguishing architectural touches that gave it its Japaneseness. Many office buildings, apartment blocks and factories in Tokyo are not only drab and uninteresting; they're drab and uninteresting in the same ways that similar buildings in Berlin or Pittsburgh are. There's nothing distinctively Japanese (or German or American) about them.

And yet, the uniformity is far from total. Different peoples do leave their differing imprints on modern artifacts and ways. The Japanese, in particular, have given modernity a special fillip. There is, it seems, a Japanese way to do everything.

Take vending machines. Every country has them. But in Japan, they're out in the open on public streets, where other countries would not dare put them for fear of robberies. And they offer beer and whiskey, which other countries avoid for fear of leading minors astray. And they offer syrupy canned coffee and concoctions with names like Pocari Sweat, which other countries might consider undrinkable.

Taxicabs are another example. Again, every country has them. But Japan's taxi culture is nonetheless unique, with its automatically opening doors and its doilies over the seats.

Then there's Japanese baseball, which is very much like American baseball, except for all the things that are different, like cheerleaders. There's Tabasco sauce, which appears on the table automatically with the salt and pepper at so many Japanese cafes even though it's seen much less often in similar settings in other countries. There's the handkerchief, which in Japan is used to dry the hands or mop the brow but never to blow the nose.

We could go on and on. But rather than do that, we've assembled a group of stories that illustrate some particularly offbeat examples of modernity with a Japanese twist. They offer a message of hope to those concerned about the preservation of local culture.

* * *

Japan's Christmas Favors Fried Chicken and Spooning

EDITOR'S NOTE: The Japanese love traditions, even other peoples' traditions. They often have their own ways of observing those traditions, however. Here is a look at Christmas, Japanese style. If you need more information on how the Japanese put their own unique stamp on everything, just ask Uncle Chimney.

TOKYO—Many young Japanese men and women will spend Christmas Eve eating fast-food fried chicken and—if they are lucky—locked in a passionate embrace at one of Tokyo's finer hotels.

Japanese boys and girls will also eat fried chicken—if they are lucky—and receive presents.

Christmas in this Buddhist nation, you see, has nothing to do with celebrating the birth of Jesus or singing "Silent Night" or gathering together with family to feast on roast turkey and plum pudding. This holiday is an opportunity to indulge in a Western rite but in a distinctly Japanese way. In recent years, "Christmas" flourishes and activities have been introduced so successfully that the holiday has become a really big deal.

Singles, for example, have bought into the concept that Christmas is for lovers, a notion introduced a few years back by a Japanese pop star.

> *Those without dates on Christmas Eve can try "Single Bells parties" at discos.*

Trendy magazines took up the idea and now have detailed instructions on how to spend Dec. 24 (the eve, not the following day, being the magical moment). "Here's our Christmas dating style," announces Checkmate, a publication "for fashion-conscious young men." Some suggestive suggestions from magazines: a five-course dinner at a fancy French restaurant, a helicopter ride around Tokyo Bay and a night in a first-class hotel.

"Ideally, I want to go to a hotel overlooking the sea, after spending the day at (Tokyo) Disneyland," says Miwa Hidaka, a 19-year-old student. But lack of a suitable partner, she says with a shrug, may prevent her from the romantic adventure.

Even if she had a date, however, she might find herself locked out of her particular dream room. At the glitzy Daiichi Hotel Tokyo Bay, near an amusement park, all 427 rooms have been reserved for Christmas Eve since the beginning of last January, says Keiko Tajima, a hotel spokeswoman. Never mind that the cheapest twin room costs $270; some love-stricken men take temporary night jobs to earn enough cash. Others, who presumably have the money, pray to Uncle Chimney for courage to confess their love.

Of course, Uncle Chimney, a version of Santa found on Christmas mugs and cards and the like, isn't infallible, and even the most financially prepared lover can face disappointment. Hiroyuki Ichiki, 24, says one of his friends booked a hotel months in advance, and even ordered a huge, custom-made cake. Then his girlfriend dropped him.

Similar tragedies deterred 10% of the customers from showing up last year at the Daiichi Hotel. This year, the hotel asked for confirmations. Other hotels request payment in advance.

The follow-the-crowd mentality can get rather tedious at times. So An-An, one of the cutting-edge women's fashion magazines, called recently for a little more originality—inviting boyfriends over to homemade chicken stewed with prunes, for example.

Still, for some young people, Japan's pre-Christmas pressure is much like finding yourself dateless before the final school dance. "I shall flee" to a solitary vacation in Europe, says a 29-year-old man, who works at a publishing company. "The last thing I want is to be caught drinking alone in my room."

But there are some nice alternatives for the brave who decide to stay. Dateless men and women can attend "Single Bells parties" at Tokyo discos. Others can reserve seats for performances of Beethoven's Ninth Symphony, considered very Western and very Christmasy.

For the younger set, Christmas is a day to receive a present. (At New Year's relatives traditionally give children cash.) Despite a recent slowdown in the general buying binge, Nikkei Gifts, a monthly magazine, expects sales of Christmas gifts and ornaments to grow about 20% from last year's $5.23 billion. One hot item in stores this year is a $280 sweater emblazoned with a picture of "Captain Santa," clad in shorts and boat shoes.

Youngsters may get treated to a Western meal, too, if their parents line up early enough for Kentucky Fried Chicken's

$29 "Christmas Barrel" (10 pieces of chicken, five containers of ice cream, plus salad).

"We're trying to inform customers that if they make reservations, they can secure their chicken," and not have to line up for two hours, says Shinji Kagiya, manager of a Kentucky Fried Chicken outlet in northern Tokyo. Nationwide sales on Christmas Eve last year reached $14.7 million, says the company's Japanese unit, or about five times that of an average day.

"I don't know why it has to be chicken," complains Hidemi Maejima, a 21-year-old who has spent her last four Christmases taking chicken orders. Actually, the reasons are simple: Some Japanese view fried chicken as an alternative to turkey, which isn't consumed here much. And many people think Kentucky Fried's jolly-looking Colonel Sanders resembles Santa Claus.

Another food tradition is a "French-style" strawberry shortcake with a plastic fir tree stuck on top. It was introduced 70 years ago by Fujiya Co., a Japanese confectionery concern, as a kind of variant of plum pudding. Guilt-ridden fathers would often take this treat home to children after staying out late drinking in hostess bars. Cake-shop staffers, shivering in the cold night air, use megaphones to hawk the cakes to drunken businessmen.

The origins of celebrating Christmas Eve in Japan are unclear. Some people say it dates from the 1930s, well before the U.S. occupation following World War II. Holiday merchandising started coming into its own in the 1960s.

This year, however, there are signs that one real American way of celebrating Christmas may be coming to town. The Western U.S. Agricultural Trade Association recently delivered 700 pine trees shipped from Montana and Oregon, with a package of tinsel and ornaments included.

Debbie Howard, president of Japan Market Network

Association, who helped bring the trees over, says that Japanese formerly always bought artificial trees, mostly 25-centimeter-tall desktop models, if they bought trees at all.

The fresh flora first had to get through customs. Officers were initially reluctant to let in the trees, which require extensive fumigation. The association insisted that the trees are a kind of harmless "freshly cut flower," priced at $155 a "blossom."

— YUMIKO ONO

December 18, 1991

* * *

Japan's Sunset Expert Shines Light on Commentators

EDITOR'S NOTE: Sometimes what distinguishes Japan's approach to modernity is simply the extremes to which the Japanese carry things. People in many societies exchange name cards, for example, but in Japan it is an obsession. People everywhere keep track of where their country ranks on a variety of scales, from gross national product to longevity, but in Japan it is a fetish. And "experts" sound off on television everywhere, but the main character of this story might have a difficult time selling his expertise outside Japan.

TOKYO—The sun always sets on Masayuki Yui's empire. If it didn't, he would be out of a job.

Mr. Yui is a sunset expert. On TV and in magazines, he

rates sunsets, analyzes them and comments on how they relate to travel, nature, science, spirituality, music and perfume.

Recently, he has been predicting a bright future for sunsets in the Western Pacific: "The dust from the volcano in the Philippines stretched out the red waves" in the spectrum, he says, meaning, "for the next year or two, beautiful." The volcano he is talking about is Mount Pinatubo.

> *But how does one become a commentator? How does a fellow establish himself as an expert on college girls?*

Mr. Yui, however, is no deep-voiced TV astronomer like Carl Sagan, no prolific polymath print man like Isaac Asimov. In fact, Mr. Yui doesn't know all that much more about meteorology or physics than does the average actor, which is what he is when he isn't being a sunset expert. He has never been a scientist, but he has played a samurai in the movies.

Still, people pay him $2,256 an hour to sound off about sunsets. At the age of 44, Mr. Yui is a star in the firmament of Japanese *hyoronka,* commentators, armchair experts on everything from philately to Phoenicians. They are in constant demand with Japan's voracious media.

As elsewhere, news in Japan isn't truly news until somebody goes on the air to reflect on it. On arcane matters such as nuclear proliferation and corn futures, the press and television everywhere turn to academics and experts with credentials. But it seems peculiar to Japan that ordinary people can so easily become established commentators on narrow, even bizarre, topics. One man specializes in tango bands, one woman in school uniforms. Some hyoronka are experts on . . . hyoronka.

"The Directory of Commentators" lists experts on "haircology" (hyoronka Mikiko Nishio says that "from the quality of a person's hair, you can tell a person's character"). There are experts on how dinosaurs fought, experts on unidentified flying objects.

The directory names 4,500 supposed experts, but nowhere near all the hyoronka actively mouthing off in Japan. Just ask Yasunori Okadome, the author of "Mass Communication Guerrilla" and a self-styled commentator on commentators. He says that in this country one can buy "2,388 magazines and lots more specialty publications, five national newspapers, maybe 120 regional newspapers. Suppose each has 10 commentators. They overlap some—that makes 23,000 commentators."

Says Reugene Nishikawa, a marketing consultant and commentator for all seasons: "We've got many television channels, magazines and newspapers. They all need someone."

In his student days, Mr. Nishikawa was a media expert on college girls, but, he says, he has since branched out to "cars, resorts, fashion, restaurants. I myself enjoy these."

But how does one become a commentator? How does a fellow establish himself as an expert on college girls?

Self-promotion is one way. Mr. Nishikawa has been unabashedly cultivating media connections since his days as campus-magazine editor at Hitotsubashi University in Tokyo. "Almost all the creative people in Japan are my friends," he says. "If they're in trouble for a comment, they call me." Not all hyoronka are as wide-ranging or as plugged in as Mr. Nishikawa, or as underqualified as Mr. Yui. Some do exhaustive research. In studying Japanese massage parlors, commentator Keiichi Hirooka visited more than 200 *toruko,* as they are known. His bath book sold 180,000 copies, and he got a lot of exposure on late-night TV.

Mikio Miyake, author of "26 Ways to Win 50 Million Yen,"

conducted a survey of over 4,000 Japanese lottery winners.

"I spent 13 years studying this," says Mr. Miyake, who won a million yen himself in 1981 and figures he has since lost more than a third of his winnings on more lottery tickets. "I'm on television and radio whenever there's a big lottery," he says. His best advice: Use a lucky number. He also recommends consulting fortunetellers and taking advantage of a run of luck. Dreaming about snakes is a lucky sign, he says.

Mr. Yui, idol of the twilights, did do some homework before he started declaiming on sunsets. And before he was an actor, he ran a sporting-goods business.

In 1982, Mr. Yui answered a newspaper ad and as a result landed a big part in the Akira Kurosawa film *"Kagemusha."* But Mr. Yui's bio was too drab for the movies, he says, "so I decided I liked sunsets, and called myself a sunset critic. It was a joke on how people call themselves experts here," he recalls. Then he, too, got taken seriously.

Sources of Inspiration

"Asahi Television called me up and asked me to be a critic on sunsets. I laughed at them." But when the giggling stopped, he says, he decided to read up on sundown. He took some snapshots, meditated and called the TV people back. From then on it was a short trip to forming the Y.U.I. Sunset Office and an affiliate called Sunset Films.

The office is equipped with the tools of his trade, which include books, celestial posters, computers, videos, a Rock-Ola jukebox and a supply of Early Times Kentucky whiskey. Mr. Yui hangs out there when he isn't otherwise engaged making movies or whatnot. "I've appeared on TV, given lectures, made commercials, gone overseas. I've watched a lot of sunsets," he says.

He earns between 100,000 yen ($752) and 300,000 yen for a TV appearance, something less for his ruminations in magazines. For all the money Mr. Yui makes at it, though, he still considers sunset comments a labor of love.

"You feel good looking at sunsets. It would be great if you could spend the whole day looking at sunsets," he says. In lectures, "I take the opportunity to tell people to look at the sunset, and not lead such a hassled life."

Revering Authority

Less ethereal hyoronka agree it's a mission, not a job. And in a society in which it's often rude to press one's views, hyoronka arguably fill a useful role. They take responsibility for their subject, and help get the conversational ball rolling. Commentator-on-commentators Mr. Okadome sees a grander message in the phenomenon, as a good commentator should.

"Until 1945, we believed the emperor was a god," he says. "For us, it's easy to believe in something absolutely. Commentators are absolute authorities." Wary of the common title, Mr. Okadome likes to be identified on TV as an author or an editor, not a commentator.

And as for Mr. Yui, he may have started off cynical, but he has warmed to his place in the sun. "I want to make domes on the tops of big mountains that will hold 2,000 people, where they can enjoy 360-degree sunsets, while they listen to music and smell great fragrances."

The idea puts Mr. Yui in a contemplative mood. "You know, when you look at a sunset, some of the rays stop on you, some go around you," he says. "If they can see the sunset on Jupiter, my shadow would be in it. It makes me a part of the universe."

A silence fills the room. Not bad, someone says. Mr. Yui smiles. "Yes," he says, "that's why I'm the sunset critic."

— QUENTIN HARDY

April 1, 1992

Japan's Soft-Sell Female Insurance Agents Push Hard

EDITOR'S NOTE: There's always a better way. But what's "better" depends on your point of view. If you're the president of an insurance company, the following might provide some interesting pointers. If you're the kind who seems to attract insurance agents as friends, perhaps you'll feel grateful that your agent isn't as "sticky" as many of those in Japan. Either way, this is a lesson in how the Japanese can even put their special imprint on something as seemingly pedestrian as life insurance.

TOKYO—For over a year, the middle-aged woman pursued Tamizo Kimura, a 30-year-old securities analyst and father of two.

She found excuses almost every week to visit him at his office at Yamaichi Securities Co. She took him wristwatch calendars and other tokens of her esteem. And when they chanced to meet in the subway, Mr. Kimura recalls, "she greeted me with a very deep bow."

Eventually she got her man. Today Mr. Kimura pays the equivalent of $57 a month on the $143,500 life-insurance policy she sold him. He says he bought the policy "as a hedge against uncertainty," but he concedes he wouldn't have purchased it from a man. "In the case of females, we tend to lower our guard," Mr. Kimura says. "Even if we feel she is too sticky, we try to be generous."

Softest Sort

That's life insurance, Japanese style. Most of the salesmen are women. Many of the sales result from the softest sort of soft-sell techniques.

Insurance people carry the pursuit of sales to the point of serving as personal advisers, in some cases even arranging marriages.

As in other countries, insurance salespersons in Japan pay a potential client frequent visits during which they talk about a lot of things besides insurance. Unlike their counterparts elsewhere, Japanese insurance people carry the pursuit to the point of serving as personal advisers, in some cases even arranging marriages.

Lining up mates "is part of my service to my customers," says Mutsuko Inoue of Sumitomo Mutual Life Insurance Co. She has helped match a number of couples and has several other as-yet-unfulfilled match-making requests.

Such saleswomanship has helped turn Japan into the world's best-insured country. Life insurance in force here at the end of 1978, the latest full year for which figures are available, amounted to $20,200 per capita, compared with $13,124 in the U.S. About 75% of Japanese households have life insurance.

The insurance payments help provide Japan with capital to build its industries. As of March 1980, life-insurance companies accounted for 4.9% of funds available at all Japanese financial institutions.

The life-insurance boom and the coming of age of the Japanese insurance woman are post-World-War-II phenomena.

Before the war, life insurance wasn't so popular and insurance women were almost nonexistent. Even today, middle-aged and older women don't easily find jobs in most other industries. Males dominate the labor force, and sex discrimination is widely accepted as natural.

Insurance is the exception. After the war, the government urged insurers to hire women so as to help the nation's many war widows support themselves. The companies responded and the hiring of women has become a tradition. Industry officials estimate that 80% of the 336,000 insurance salespeople in Japan are women.

Kazuko Shibata, one of Japan's top insurance saleswomen—she earned more than $190,000 at it last year—says the job's main attraction is the chance to add to family income. She says she and her husband have built three houses over the years, mostly with her earnings. (They live in one and rent the other two.) Mr. Shibata is a manager of a small company that supplies shampoo, hair dryers and the like to beauty salons.

"If we relied only on the income of my husband," she says, "we couldn't have built a single house without borrowing from the bank."

Insurance companies like having women on their sales staffs. They say they find it hard to attract top-quality males because selling insurance isn't prestigious work, but bright women are eager for insurance jobs.

Then, too, the companies note, women don't meet with as much sales resistance as men do. Housewives aren't as reluctant to answer the door when it's a woman knocking, and men find it harder to reject a saleswoman's entreaties.

Seduction Stories
There have been stories of insurance women seducing customers to make sales, but the insurance companies insist such

accounts are fictitious. The truth, says one company official, is that "females are more tenacious and diligent than men" in selling insurance. "In a man-to-man situation, if the potential customer says, 'No, I am not interested,' that's it. The salesman won't go any further." With women, it isn't so, the official says.

One example of female tenaciousness and diligence is the marriage-arranging technique of Sumitomo Life's Miss Inoue and many of her competitors. In November 1979, Miss Inoue was approached by a 28-year-old construction-company employee who had bought insurance from her in the past. He was looking for a wife, he said.

Knowing that the customer's marriage could lead to even more insurance business, Miss Inoue swung into action. Her first thought was to match the man with another customer, a cosmetics demonstrator. As it happened, the demonstrator had a boyfriend. But she also had a 23-year-old girlfriend, another cosmetics demonstrator, who was single and looking. Miss Inoue interviewed the girlfriend, and "after I became convinced that she was recommendable, I did it. I arranged it." The couple is doing very well now, she adds.

Despite such heartwarming tales, making a living selling insurance is just as tough here as anywhere else. While some saleswomen make $48,000 a year or more in commission, many others just get by. So many, in fact, that the government in 1974 issued an "administrative instruction" urging insurers to employ sales staffers full time and to pay them at least a minimum wage. The minimum varies by location and now is about $335 a month in Tokyo.

The fierce competition leads to high turnover. In the fiscal year ended March 31, 1980, a total of 150,414 salespeople left the life-insurance companies' employ while 158,329 entered it. Among those who left is 54-year-old Kazuko Kamikakeuchi. She says that after two years selling insurance in Nagoya, she had used up all her personal contacts and didn't have anyone else to sell to.

"Personal contacts" often means friends and relatives. One insurance buyer, Wahei Sakurai, 29, says the only reason he purchased his $143,500 policy was that "my sister was then working with a life-insurance company."

The insurers are aware of Japan's Mr. Sakurais. They note that in a 1979 survey, 41% of the respondents said they bought insurance because of "personal connections" with the insurance agent, compared with 42% who said they "needed" insurance. But the companies cite this personal factor as just another reason for using women.

"The brand image of life insurance depends on the image of the salesperson," not the company's name, says an official at a major life-insurance company. As a result, he says, the role of women in Japan's insurance industry will grow even more important in the future.

— MASAYOSHI KANABAYASHI

March 28, 1981

* * *

Pampered Pets Lap Up Life of Luxury in Japan

EDITOR'S NOTE: Perhaps it's because California and Japan are about the same size and face each other across the Pacific. Perhaps it's because they're both frequently rumbled by earthquakes. Or perhaps California was Japan in a previous incarnation—or vice versa. Whatever the reason, the two places share a penchant for being on the cutting edge of some of the world's wackier trends. Or are private yoga lessons for poodles common everywhere?

KINUGAWA—After traveling 160 kilometers from Tokyo to one of Japan's most popular hot-spa resorts, Mary decides she doesn't like bathing outdoors, especially with male company. She takes one dip in the steaming water, then springs up, clutching the edge of the tub. She glances indignantly at Harry, who sits relaxed, head back in the water, eyes closed.

Mary, an eight-month-old miniature spaniel, and Harry, a two-year-old chihuahua, are spending a relaxing weekend at the Kinugawa Kokusai Hotel's "pets-only, mixed-bathing" outdoor spa. After the bath, they will get a thorough blow-dry, and then chow down a low-fat dinner of boiled chicken and milk, at the same table as their owners.

Such are the lengths to which Japanese pet lovers go to pamper their pooches.

Californians may have their dog cemeteries and cat psychics, but in the past few years, Japanese pet freaks have become every bit as eccentric, creating a $2-billion-a-year industry. Goods and services now available to Japan's 12 million dogs and cats include diapers, bikinis, dating services, weddings, yoga and funerals.

"This pet boom is absurd," says Katsumi Hoshino, a lecturer on changing social trends at Tsukuba University. "There are more businesses for pets than for people."

The cause of all this is simple: Some Japanese have more money than they know what to do with. Few can afford to buy housing in Japan's overheated real-estate market, so some spend the surplus yen on canned oxygen (used by sports buffs and others) and electric nail shavers. Others, particularly middle-aged women, buy $1,900 Maltese dogs or $3,800 Scottish fold cats, give them American names, which they think are cute, and then shower the little darlings with luxuries.

"Whenever I see cute pet clothes, I keep wanting to buy them," says Kinue Gunji, a housewife living in the south of Tokyo. "Sure they cost money. But I love my dog more than my child." Mrs. Gunji is staying at the spa with her daughter, her husband, and her Pomeranian, Shelley, who gets a monthly medical checkup, and was recently treated to a new set of rain boots.

"I love my dog more than my child."

Hotel owner Keiko Akutsu began offering pet lodging and meals last year, after she took a trip to Europe and was impressed by the welcome many hotels there extended to animals. Expanding on the European concept, Mrs. Akutsu charges people $110 a night to stay at her hotel, and allows their pets to stay with them for an extra $4. Her hotel's revenues have nearly doubled.

"The owners are so pleased when we treat the pets like people," says the 55-year-old Mrs. Akutsu, who even has little futon mattresses for the pets. Animal guests, who tend to arrive wearing hats and dresses, are referred to as "little boys" and "little girls." Owners are discreetly handed a plastic pickup bag and a packet of tissues before they go for a walk.

These boys and girls are free to socialize in the lounge beside the pet souvenir shop, while their owners chat. Squeezed into a tight jump suit, Chuji, a chubby male Pomeranian, bounces off the table, flapping the ribbons tied around his ears. Two of his buttons have burst. "We have a jump suit just like that one," says Mrs. Gunji, the devoted owner of Shelley. "But ours has a little pocket to put tissues in."

Chuji and Mary rub noses, and their owners coo in delight. Shingo, a one-kilogram chihuahua wrapped in a red kilted vest, is jealous. Seeking attention, he strolls over to the bar and urinates on the carpet, making Mrs. Akutsu rush over with a can of deodorant spray. His owner, a middle-aged woman in pink pajamas, gives him a little slap, then cuddles him tightly.

Those looking for more things to put on the dog will enjoy the Osaka pet fair that began this month. Along with pet clothes, wigs and good-luck charms, there were $380,000 cats that pranced around wearing $6,000 necklaces. And there is even a wedding on the schedule. On Sept. 22, two Shetland sheep dogs, one dressed in a tuxedo and the other in a wedding dress, are to exchange collars in front of a human "priest," as bow-tied St. Bernards and Pomeranians will likely watch and wag.

Actually, the groom was lucky to have found a bride. In Japan, where many pet owners live in apartments, most male house pets can't sneak out at night, and thus have no chance to meet girls.

They end their lives single and sad, says Isoroku Kimura, a Tokyo pet-shop owner. He felt so sorry for them that last year he set up a pet dating service. Twenty dogs, each of whose owners have dished out snapshots, resumes and $75 per date, have high hopes for the coming mating season over the next few months.

Even pets' everyday food and clothing are becoming more trendy. At Adachiya, a pet fashion boutique in Tokyo's Asakusa district, a baseball uniform, with cap and socks, hangs next to a raincoat and a dress with huge sunflower patterns. (Sunflowers are also current fashion for human girls in Japan.)

"We sometimes wonder if these things are really necessary," says Yoshio Iida, an Adachiya executive. But the tiny store sold 170 pet garments one cold winter day. The clothes, priced $30 and up, are made in all sizes, to fit anything from chihuahuas to Great Danes. A simpler T-shirt, jump suit or cotton kimono is recommended for sharp-nailed cats. There are also a red bikini for the beach, a knapsack for the mountains, a $300 kimono and a $7,600 white mink coat for special photo-taking occasions.

Sogo department store in Yokohama prepares elaborate take-out meals for pets. The most popular, says a store official, is the $75 pet steak dinner of premium rare beef, unsalted ham, sausages and cheese, and white chocolate for dessert. Yasuaki Ohmori, a Tokyo high-school teacher, confesses to having stolen a bite of his dachshund's meal, a meat dish in a special sauce. "It was quite tasty," he says in embarrassment.

When too much rich food starts showing as flab, Fido can turn to jogging machines and yogurt made especially for dogs. At Japan Trimming School, pets can take a 45-minute private yoga lesson for $35: An instructor personally stretches them into 15 poses, intended to improve blood circulation and relax muscles. (Concentration is said to be essential, so distracting observers aren't allowed.) Although most students are canines, someone once brought a rabbit for a stretch.

After the prized pet eventually passes away, a funeral service will cremate the pet right outside the owner's door. Jippo Corp., a truck company, sends a young woman ceremony director in the "Pet Angel Service" truck. Clad in a pink jump suit to give the event a rosier image, she instructs tearful owners to place flowers on the pink altar, next to the truck's incinerator. "Thank you for taking care of me up till now," says a recorded woman's voice. The ashes are placed in a candy jar.

A more symbolic ritual proceeds in a planetarium-like dome in the basement of a western Tokyo pet shop. Mourners gaze upward at a $520,000 computer-generated image of a galaxy, while music blares. A pulsing blob of light in a clear pyramid, meant to represent the pet's soul, shoots a spark of light into a star.

"There," says the funeral director. "The pet has gone back to the land of stars."

— YUMIKO ONO

September 13, 1988

* * *

In Japan, a Hole in One Means a Hole in the Pocket

> *EDITOR'S NOTE: Strange things can happen to games when they migrate. Cricket and baseball are a good example. So are rugby and American football. But surely, you say, golf is golf no matter where you go. Well, yes and no. The rules may be the same, but local customs can differ widely. The Japanese, for example, buy insurance to protect themselves against what golfers in most other places would consider their finest moment on the links.*

TOKYO—Insurance salesman Akira Anzai will never forget the misery he felt on the 173-yard (52-meter) third hole at Japan's Kuju Lakeside Golf Course. There, on a cloudy day in 1983, he watched his tee shot fly straight to the green, bounce once and disappear.

He had hit a hole in one.

"The whole world went black," Mr. Anzai recalls.

Hitting a hole in one can be one of the sweetest pleasures of a golfer's career. But in Japan it is dreadful. The unfortunate golfer is expected to throw a party and to send presents—to friends, to co-workers and to everyone who witnessed the feat. The cost can run into thousands of dollars.

> *"I signed up for hole-in-one insurance and now am playing golf with peace of mind," says a Japanese golfer.*

Entertaining Customers

About 10 million Japanese play golf, more than one in every 10 adults. The most avid golfers are businessmen, who use the sport to entertain customers. It is part of what the Japanese call *otsukiai,* relationship building. A survey found that the average golfer spends more than $100 a month on the pastime—for clubs, fees, clothes and such—not counting hole-in-one presents.

Nothing could be more embarrassing than to hit a hole in one in front of a customer, and then fail to pony up with a good present.

But the Japanese, who invented the problem, have also come up with a solution: hole-in-one insurance. For a fee of $5 to $10 a year, the Japanese golfer can buy a policy that will pay off as much as $2,000 should the unthinkable occur.

To collect on a claim, you must send the insurance company receipts proving that you spent money on presents and parties. And you need to send in forms attesting to your lucky shot, signed by the club, your golfing companions and the caddie. (In Japan, almost all caddies are women, known as *kyadii-san*. They wear large bonnets and move the clubs around on electric handcarts.)

Some golfers find out about hole-in-one insurance the hard way. Shigeji Suzuki, a certified public accountant, was playing golf with a group of local notables late last November.

"It was the end of the year, and I was thinking it has been a good year, without any serious mishaps either personal or in business," says Mr. Suzuki. Then he dropped a 147-yard (134-meter) shot with his No. 3 wood on the eighth hole. And he had no insurance.

"At the moment of the hole in one, I was elated and thought, 'I did it!'" says Mr. Suzuki. "Then I thought, 'Oh, no!' I began to worry about the contents of my wallet."

His wife shared his concern. "What a rotten thing to do," she told him when he arrived home. She knew her golf. First, Mr. Suzuki had to tip two caddies $20 each. Then, the Suzukis paid $850 for 15 gold pens, which were engraved and sent to Mr. Suzuki's closest friends and business associates and to his golf partners. The couple spent an additional $400 on 100 golf towels, printed with his name and the details of his feat. The towels went to the B-list of friends and associates. At the end of January, Mr. Suzuki laid out $850 to rent the Club Fushimi, a hostess bar in one of Tokyo's nightclub districts, where he entertained his friends.

Mr. Suzuki has mended his ways. "I was told that things that happen once may happen twice," he says. "So, although it is a bit late, I signed up for hole-in-one insurance and now am playing golf with peace of mind."

One Big Party

"The Japanese will use any excuse for a party," says Mowa Setsu, an 86-year-old golf historian and consultant who has played the game since 1925. "It isn't just holes in one. They also give out presents and have a big party when they shoot their ages, that is, when someone's golf score for 18 holes adds up to his age."

So far, insurance companies don't offer shoot-your-age insurance. In fact, they are losing money on hole-in-one insurance.

"The trouble with hole-in-one insurance is what we call moral risk," explains an insurance agent. "Especially in the areas south and west of Tokyo—in Osaka, Kobe and Kyushu—where golf courses aren't so crowded. The players can get awfully close to the caddies. They may finish up a round of golf and decide they want to have a party. So they give the caddie $40, and get her to attest that one of them hit a hole in one. Since the maximum amount you can collect is relatively small, it hardly pays to investigate a claim." The agent says he thinks hole-in-one insurance may be withdrawn.

A spokesman for Tokio Marine & Fire Insurance Co., one of Japan's largest casualty companies, denies any plans to abandon the coverage. But it is true that the company raised rates by 80% a year ago. It may even have to raise them again, says Takashi Ienaka, a Tokio Marine official, because "the amount going out still is much bigger than the amount coming in." He estimates that golfers hit holes in one on three out of every 10,000 shots, but he says the company seems to be paying out more often than that.

"Of course, we can't say there isn't any cheating," Mr. Ienaka explains. "Only God knows who is cheating and who isn't. But we take the view that we must trust our policy-holders."

Golf experts here speculate that the tradition of hole-in-one parties and gifts grows from the widespread notion that good luck should be shared.

"If you keep the luck all for yourself, you will be thrown under a curse," the chairman of Nippon Steel Corp., Japan's largest steel company, told a Japanese golf magazine recently.

The Nippon Steel executive, Eishiro Saito, hit a hole in one while golfing with the chairman of Sumitomo Electric Corp. He thereupon sent 500 golf umbrellas to friends and associates.

Tokyo department stores say the most popular presents are towels. But golfers also buy ball markers, drinking glasses, leather score-card holders, tie pins, key holders, bag tags and lacquer trays, usually engraved with details of the shot. A Japanese confectioner has since 1926 sold "hole in one" candies made of sweet bean paste and shaped like golf balls.

When the president of Suntory Ltd., Japan's largest brewery and liquor company, hit a hole in one, he had 1,000 golf-ball-shaped whiskey bottles made, filled them with his best liquor and sent them to one and all.

Mr. Anzai, the insurance salesman, had a special problem with his hole in one. When it happened to him he was in the company of other insurance men and customers. And he, of all people, owned just $400 in hole-in-one insurance.

"I was hoping that it wasn't really a hole in one," he recalls. "I looked around on the green, hoping to see the ball, but there wasn't anything white there. Then I noticed there was something white in the hole. My feelings were complex."

After the obligatory spending spree, Mr. Anzai contacted his company and arranged to increase his coverage.

— E.S. BROWNING

August 23, 1985

* * *

Tora-San Movies Recall a More Compassionate Japan

EDITOR'S NOTE: The Japanese think of themselves as a "wet," "sticky," emotional people, not cool and rational, as they imagine Westerners to be. Of course, a people's self-image is often distorted, and some foreign students of Japan question this one. For a sense of why the Japanese view themselves the ways they do, consider their fondness for one of the great all-time sentimental screen heroes, Tora-san.

KATSUSHIKA WARD, Tokyo—This is where Tora-san lives.

You can tell by the posters—some of which bear his name, others his face—on the shops jammed along the lane from Shibamata Station to Taishakuten, a Shinto shrine in this working-class section of the city.

Amid the commercial warren 58-year-old Tadao Osuga glances up from the rice that he is shoveling down in his restaurant. A neighboring shopkeeper, apologizing for the interruption, explains that a foreign journalist wants to ask about the main character in what is, according to the Guinness Book of Records, the world's longest movie series.

'What Do We Think?'

Mr. Osuga grunts assent, pushes aside his bowl and motions the visitor to sit down. Having examined the journalist's credentials, Mr. Osuga folds his arms, tilts his head and purses his lips: "What do we think of Tora-san?"

As vice chairman of the street's merchants' association, Mr. Osuga is one of the few people here willing to field such questions for the record. "There used to be lots of guys like

Tora-san around. Down in the Yamanote area (Tokyo's inner circle of posher neighborhoods) they'd consider that type outlandish. But out here they weren't unusual." Mr. Osuga, whose family has run this establishment for 100 years, declares, "Tora-san's movies aren't false."

Tora-san is the protagonist of *"Otoko Wa Tsurai Yo,"* literally "It's Tough Being a Man," a series of films whose 37 installments began in 1969.

> *Tora-san "talks like a gangster, but he's gentle inside. You don't know whether to laugh or cry."*

Played by Kiyoshi Atsumi, a former professional comic storyteller, Tora-san is a ne'er-do-well peddler who wanders around Japan in a fedora and a plaid suit. His double-breasted jacket often hangs unbuttoned, revealing a long-sleeved undershirt and a wide woolen stomach band of the sort favored by old men and certain rough customers. Like Charlie Chaplin's tramp, says the series' director and main writer, Yoji Yamada, Tora-san "is low on the social ladder but has great pride."

At a time when many Japanese worry that modern prosperity is stripping life of the *ninjo,* human feelings, at the core of personal relationships, Tora-san is a reminder of the way things were.

"He talks like a gangster, but he's gentle inside. You don't know whether to laugh or cry," says a 68-year-old fan at a theater in Tokyo's prosperous Shibuya district. "You don't find people like that anymore."

Says Mr. Osuga, the restaurateur, "There's no compassion anymore. If people see someone lying on the street in Ginza (a fashionable Tokyo shopping district), they won't bother to see if he's all right. They don't want to get involved. They don't want to give up their time. Tora-san would wake the guy up, ask him what's wrong, give him some money."

Predictable Plots

For Tora-san aficionados, the predictability of the movie plots is half the fun of watching them unfold.

Tora-san meets a beautiful woman in distress. He cheers her with his comic bravado and selflessly helps her cope, all the while falling into deep but unspoken love. He introduces her to the folks back in Shibamata, maybe even helps her find a steady job. His family, against all better judgment, begins to hope that he has finally found Miss Right.

Then, the inevitable: The woman finds happiness elsewhere, usually in the form of another man. She thanks Tora-san, as if he were a brother. He gallantly wishes her well and hides his disappointment. The music swells; the journey resumes.

Each Tora-san film is prefaced by a dream scene that hints vaguely at the main story. In December, with the opening just 11 days away, Mr. Yamada is shooting the final segment of the dream scene for the latest installment, subtitled *"Shiawase no Aoi Tori,"* or "The Blue Bird of Happiness."

The scene is staged at Shochiku Co.'s 50-year-old studio in Ofuna, just south of Yokohama.

Amid craggy artificial rocks and dry-ice mist, Tora-san's sister, Sakura, and brother-in-law, Hiroshi, both in bedraggled hiking gear, call out for Tora-san to turn back and abandon what has been, for them, a brutal and apparently futile journey. Tora-san, bouncing out from behind the rocks in an immaculate white scarf and pith helmet and wielding a large butterfly net, insists that they will capture the "blue bird of happiness," if only they keep looking.

"Hiroshi, don't you want to be happy?" implores Tora-san.

"Happiness is something you grasp with your own hands," retorts the exasperated Hiroshi.

"But that's why we've been traveling for the past half-year," insists Tora-san. "To grasp the blue bird of happiness in our hands."

In an essay published earlier this month by a Japanese sports newspaper, Mr. Yamada, the director, writes that Tora-san's failure to marry or to settle into a respectable job is due partly to his romanticism. To take a beautiful, pure-hearted woman off her pedestal or to grapple with the practical dilemmas of the workaday world would risk spoiling the dream.

During a break in the filming, Mr. Yamada, who is 55, explains why he wants to keep making Tora-san films as long as he and the other members of the cast can.

"At first, the films were about common people's lives," says Mr. Yamada, who worked his way through Tokyo University's elite law school before joining Shochiku in 1954, in the heyday of Japan's film industry. "Things have changed enormously" since the series began, "but the films have stayed the same."

"Have the changes been for the better? Are there things that have been lost? I want the Japanese people to think about these things," says Mr. Yamada, a handsome, soft-spoken man whose longish hair is streaked with silver.

Around the corner from the Shibuya theater, in a back-alley row of hole-in-the-wall bars that date back to the early postwar era, it's apparent that many middle-aged men continue to thirst for the kind of earthy intimacy and reassurance that Tora-san's neighborhood provides.

At Bui bar, where seven stools line the narrow space between wall and counter, Shigeko Hirano dispenses keg sake, regional delicacies and blunt advice to her patrons.

"Poor, rich, fools, geniuses—anyone can appreciate Tora-san films," says Nozomi Kato, one of the intellectuals who frequent Bui. "Joy, anger, sadness, pleasure—all the basic human emotions are there. That's why the appeal is broad."

Tora-san isn't everyone's cup of tea, however. At a fondue party in an upper-middle-class Tokyo home, a couple of the guests snicker when asked if they go to Tora-san films. "Sometimes you do hear about someone's parents going to see one," says a travel agent in his 30s, "but I don't think many people our age do."

But Mr. Yamada and studio executives say the numbers of young viewers have increased steadily. The twice-yearly films are timed to coincide with two major holiday seasons: New Year, and Obon in August, when families gather to pay respects to their ancestors. The films have attracted an estimated audience of 60 million people since they began 17 years ago. In recent years the Tora-san series has accounted for roughly 20% of the feature-film revenues at Shochiku, one of Japan's leading movie makers. The 30th installment, in 1983, was the series' biggest hit thus far.

The series appears to have a certain universal appeal as well. In addition to Tora-san fan clubs in Hawaii and Los Angeles, Shochiku officials report a new one is about to start in Vienna. "The mayor of Vienna is a great Tora-san fan," says Mr. Yamada. "They've asked us to shoot a Tora-san movie on location there."

That's good news as far as Mr. Osuga is concerned. "If more people watch Tora-san films, they'll understand the Japanese heart: compassion . . ." The Shibamata restaurant owner pauses, then adds: "Well, compassion has been getting scarcer lately . . . Times have progressed too far."

— CHRISTOPHER J. CHIPELLO

January 28, 1987

SECTION THREE

ACCORDING
TO FORM

Introduction

Westerners draw a sharp distinction between form and substance. Japanese often don't. To them, form *is* substance. Or, if they admit a distinction, they don't worry much about substance. Doing things the right way, by the rules, according to form is what matters.

The visitor to Japan can see examples of this everywhere he turns. In the "salarymen" on the commuter trains practicing their golf swings with imaginary clubs, perfecting their form. In the fruits and vegetables in the markets, which must look "just so" or go unbought. In the corporate training sessions where new employees are taught precisely how low to bow. In the punctuality of subway trains, not to mention society generally. In the patient attentiveness to detail of a typical Japanese factory. In the widespread disdain for casual or sloppy clothing—except among those youngsters who deliberately wear torn jeans to affect a sloppy look, which is itself a kind of formalism. In the popularity of such form-stressing arts as bonsai, flower arranging and calligraphy.

Japan's ideographic writing system reinforces the emphasis on form. Students must spend countless hours learning the thousands of Chinese characters required for normal literacy. Not just to recognize the characters, nor even just to reproduce them in some recognizable fashion. They must learn the right way to make each stroke, and the precise order for the strokes in each character. These "right ways" promote faster and more readable penmanship and facilitate the use of dictionaries, which are of necessity indexed by stroke count. Still, the end result is to reinforce a more general societal preference for following the rules.

The fixation with form vexes some foreigners, especially longtime expatriates who know (and thus feel they are expected to heed) the intricate conventions of Japanese life. Some experience an elated sense of freedom whenever they leave the country. Wise foreigners learn not to fight the system, however. An American paper company built a new kind of rack to hold its rolls of paper while enroute to Japan. Without the rack, the rocking of the ship would sometimes lead to scuffs on the outer packaging, and Japanese customers would reject the rolls in scuffed packages even though the usefulness of the rolls themselves was unimpaired.

Another triumph of form over substance? Maybe. But in Japan, the customer wants good form, and the customer is always right.

* * *

Well-Trained Commuters Keep Tokyo Subways Running on Time

EDITOR'S NOTE: Several generations ago, visitors to the U.S. used to marvel over how well everything worked. The postal system. The trains. America's honesty and attentiveness to detail inspired admiration and confidence. Several decades ago, visitors to Japan began to notice the same kind of honesty and attentiveness to detail. But unlike the U.S., which seemed to lose these virtues as it reached more advanced stages of development, Japan remains obsessed with making sure the trains run precisely on time.

TOKYO—A subway train slips out of Higashi-Ginza Station and into a dim, gray tunnel. Motorman Osamu Igarashi sits erect in his chair, his eyes zeroing in on the signals ahead.

Obeying the rules he learned in driver training, he points at each sign with a white-gloved hand and quietly chants its meaning: "Automatic proceed," he twangs. "Speed limit 50." Mr. Igarashi eases the train into Shimbashi Station, where hundreds of workers and schoolchildren stand in tidy rows behind floor markings that indicate precisely where the doors will open. It is 5:13:50 p.m.

> ## *"We're a little late," says Mr. Igarashi, stealing a glance at his stopwatch. "About eight seconds."*

"We're a little late," says Mr. Igarashi, stealing a glance at his stopwatch. "About eight seconds."

In the Tokyo area, millions of rail commuters can count on reaching their destination at pretty much the same minute every day, and that says as much about the Japanese as it does about their trains. Sure, thorough maintenance and high-tech gizmos help, but the real secret is a nation that loves to follow the rules. "It's people that delay the trains," says Shoji Yanagawa, a spokesman for Tokyo's Eidan subway company. "But then again it's people that keep the trains running on time."

Call it the cult of punctuality. Motormen and conductors who work the late shift sleep at the depot, and are roused for the morning shift by pillows that automatically inflate at the appointed time. Tokyo's train system is so finely tuned that it has eliminated almost all sources of extended delay, to the point where a major cause of lateness is the "jumper," or suicide.

Initiation in the rites of punctilious passage starts early. Tokyo elementary schools teach children the basics of train riding. In the stations, riders are bombarded with messages in schoolmarmish voices: "It's dangerous, so please don't run onto the trains." (People who rush often get stuck in the closing doors, which delays departure.)

To keep straphangers from cramming into doorways, the railways lash them with a bit of shame. "We put extra workers on the platforms, and mostly they stand there and look at the passengers," says Mr. Yanagawa. "That usually works."

Rigorous, maybe, but the commuters thronging the platform at Otemachi Station one recent evening are eager adherents. "People hear the announcements, and they try to get in the train on time," says Tetsuro Yamanaka, a 28-year-old salesman. "If they don't make it, you lose 10 seconds here, 10 seconds there," he frowns. "Soon every train on the line is a minute late."

Japan's timely trains have earned an honored spot in the nation's culture. There is a genre of crime novels, for instance, in which sleuths pinpoint the movements of villains on the assumption that the trains run to the minute.

Perhaps the most famous is "Points and Lines," a 1970 novel by Seicho Matsumoto. The hero is Inspector Mihara, a tireless Tokyo policeman who spends weeks poring over train timetables. His objective: to prove it was possible for businessman Tatsuo Yasuda to make it in time to a lonely beach in southern Japan to poison a man with cyanide.

Or browse through "Motorman" by Tomomi Fujiwara, a prize-winning 1992 novel about a prompt Tokyo subway driver who has nightmares about being late: "His eye rolled down the platform like a ping-pong ball . . . He scurried to retrieve it, but looking at his stopwatch, he noticed that just 30 seconds remained until departure, so he returned to the motorman's compartment. As he was about to leave the station, though, he wondered: Isn't driving one-eyed a violation of the rules?"

It is. In addition to passing a vision test, Tokyo's aspiring subway motormen must take a concentration-measurement test that involves adding 34 columns of numbers, 3,910 sums in all. They are judged not on their raw score, but on how closely the pattern of their correct responses conforms to the "normal" curve. That is because a key to keeping the trains on time is making them run at uniform intervals, says Kinya Yamada, a 50-year-old manager for Toei, the smaller of the city's two subway companies. "So we look for people who will all do the same thing in the same way," he says.

Like Machines

Recruits go through a nine-month training course, where they study railway history and memorize a 200-page driver's manual. On the job, drivers are held to a strict code of behavior: Be polite, don't read while on duty and always wear your white gloves. Supervisors carry checklists, grading motormen on such items as position of the feet, handle gripping and timeliness. "Motormen are a little like robots," laughs Mr. Yamada. "You might as well employ machines."

Tokyo's subways do have their headaches. Walkman batteries, for instance: Some passengers discard them on the seats, and they wind up rolling into the doorways and jamming the doors. Worse still is rain gear. Umbrellas get caught in people's legs and in the doors, slowing down the passengers. During the winter, riders' overcoats eat up space, so fewer people can squeeze aboard—or be pushed aboard by platform attendants.

Then there are the suicides. In 1992, 1,032 Japanese killed themselves by lying down or leaping in front of trains.

The delay isn't so long if the jumper survives, says Toei's Mr. Yamada matter-of-factly, because station attendants whisk the injured to the hospital. But if the person dies, the crew has to wait for the police to arrive and witnesses to be identified. "Then you're talking 40, 50 minutes," he says.

The train companies are so frustrated by this intrusion into their scheduling that they sometimes fine the families of jumpers—and even base the penalty on how many passengers are delayed.

Reading About Railroads

The press, watchdog of the public interest, does its bit for timeliness by reminding readers what a nuisance a jumper can be. "Teacher Commits Suicide on Mita Line," reads a headline in Yomiuri Shimbun, "30,000 Are Delayed During Rush Hour."

Yukio Harada, a former motorman, hit a jumper in 1978. The victim, a man in his 40s, was killed; the train was held up for half an hour, and the 52-year-old Mr. Harada, now a supervisor for Toei, was given three days off to settle his nerves. He was pretty shaken that first night, he recalls calmly, "but the next day things were back to normal."

Railways say they can't do much to stop suicides. In the year through March 1992, the Toei subway, which had six "body incidents," assessed penalties of as much as 250,000 yen ($2,250). Not that it is much of a deterrent: Most Japanese don't know the fines exist, and most families refuse to pay.

Still, with a few exceptions, promptness prevails. On a recent Tuesday, Eidan says, just 13 of its 4,500 train runs fell behind by five minutes. Excluding suicides, the Eidan and Toei systems boast that they have never had a passenger die in an accident.

In case you're wondering, Inspector Mihara's hunch was right: The tireless timetable-reading gumshoe established that the businessman was indeed at the lonely beach—and did administer the poison. But the train schedules showed an even more startling truth: The killer got there by airplane.

— MICHAEL WILLIAMS

May 27, 1993

Japanese Teens Take to Street Style as Worn by Hip American Kids

EDITOR'S NOTE: People who care about form care about personal appearance. They want to dress the part, whatever the part might be. A Japanese showing up for his first tennis lesson might very well appear on court in a complete set of expensive new tennis togs—never mind that he has never hit a tennis ball before and cannot be sure he will enjoy the sport. If he stopped to analyze his own behavior, he might rationalize that looking like a tennis player is critical to being a tennis player. Fair enough—but then what is the rationale for the people in the following story?

TOKYO—Hiroshi Kaneko has a simple dream: He wants to master the look of the urban black American teenager.

Sporting a baseball cap turned backwards, the 16-year-old burrows his hands into the pockets of his baggy pants, with cuffs rumpled over his new Patrick Ewing basketball shoes.

"Black people are so cool—like Michael Jordan," says Mr. Kaneko, popping his chewing gum. He knows that from reading magazines.

In this trend-crazed country, urban American teen culture is hot at the moment.

Just as Japanese teenagers went for Mickey Mouse and Ralph Lauren polo shirts, they're now snapping up imported sneakers and T-shirts that say "Brothers" and "Black With Attitude." Japanese rap and hip-hop groups are aping the music. Teenage boys stroll the malls with the laces of their sneakers carefully untied and greet each other with a friendly "Hey man" dropped into their Japanese.

Getting the look down takes a bit of skill, confesses Kei Asai, a 19-year-old Tokyo student outfitted in a black cap, hooded jacket and Converse sneakers. "We could be wearing the same things, but black people look cooler." A few of his friends have gone to suntan parlors to darken their skin, he says. For a mere 60,000 yen ($468), a specialized barber gives them dreadlocks. (A cheaper alternative is a $37 baseball cap with fake hair sewn onto the sides.)

Teen magazines, on the cusp of urban American life styles, treat fashion shifts in street clothes as if they were covering French couture.

Elsewhere, they find stores that stock loose-fitting trousers in the red, yellow and green of Rastafarianism and the Ethiopian flag. Salespeople promise them "clothing without prejudice" and stocking caps "fresh from New York."

But why here? This, after all, is a homogeneous nation of few minorities, with no particular reputation for ethnic sensitivity. Quite the contrary. Seiroku Kajiyama, while he was justice minister in 1990, suggested that prostitutes moving into a Japanese district had the same effect as blacks moving into a predominantly white neighborhood in America. Yasuhiro Nakasone, when he was prime minister in 1986, said the presence of minorities in the U.S. was partly to blame for the decline of the nation's public schools. Outside Tokyo, there's a suntan parlor called Blacky.

Observers of fashion here say the trend has caught on because young Japanese associate American blacks with rap and rhythm and blues, musical styles immensely popular with Tokyo teenagers. Yasutomo Matsubara, the top editor at Boon, a monthly magazine for teenage boys that promotes street fashion, suggests that there is a deeper reason for the craze. Japanese teenagers are locked in a highly regimented school and social system. They feel a comradeship. "Their lives are so repressed, and they see how black people's lives are repressed." Ergo, young Japanese men step out in fashionable defiance, sporting ponytails, multiple earrings and goggles.

Whatever the reason, the interest is more in the style than in the substance of America's street culture. Teen magazines, on the cusp of urban American life styles, treat fashion shifts in street clothes as if they were covering French couture.

"Here are the main items in street fashion" for the '93 winter wardrobe, announces Check Mate, a magazine "for fashion-conscious young men." A recent issue features turtleneck sweaters that go well with hooded jackets and advises that the correct way to wear knit caps this year is "deep, almost covering your ears."

Now store owners hope the hype surrounding the new Spike Lee movie "Malcolm X," which is to open here next March, will expand the market. Mr. Lee himself stands to profit from two stores in Tokyo—called Spike's Joint—modeled on his shop in Brooklyn. They carry a variety of stuff, including T-shirts, coffee mugs and stickers. Cedar Japan, the Tokyo importing company that handles the Spike Lee merchandise, hopes to rake in $4.9 million in annual sales by opening eight more Spike's Joints over the next three years.

Young Japanese don't have to understand urban black teenage culture to enjoy its artifacts, reasons Wataru Fukui, a 22-year-old bartender. "White people discriminating against black people—for us living here, how could we understand exactly what that means?"

Indeed, some Tokyo customers buying baseball caps with

the distinctive X logo admit they thought the X stood for the Japanese heavy-metal rock band of the same name. Mr. Fukui, for his part, says he read up on Malcolm the man before plunking down $316 on a "Malcolm X World Tour" jacket and a $39 hat that says "Stay Black."

Other shoppers, too, are discriminating about what they buy. Shunya Tomota, a 21-year-old, says he is interested only in street fashion brands popular on the West Coast. "I like the clothes that white people trying to be black are wearing," he explains earnestly, the three earrings in his left ear jingling. Another editor at Boon confesses he spends a lot of time studying the album covers of rap musicians, with emphasis on their clothes.

Such zealousness puzzles some black Americans here. "Swell" Fernandez, a 24-year-old black disk jockey working in Tokyo, says he can't understand why so many Japanese want to dress like the people back home in New York. "To tell you the truth, I think it's crazy," he says. "They've got it wrong. Being black is not a fad."

On a recent weekend, Mr. Fernandez joined in a street basketball game with Osamu Arita, a 19-year-old urban-fashion fan, who affects a Michael Jackson look. Next time, though, Mr. Arita may have to make certain adjustments. Chasing a pass in his new work boots, which fashion magazines say are replacing sneakers in the U.S., he trips and goes flying across the court. Later, Mr. Arita, in a philosophical mood, wonders whether the Japanese fascination with urban American styles is "just rich people being spoiled."

If so, there are many of them. Pajaboo, a Tokyo store specializing in street fashion, does a brisk business in knit caps with a "Brooklyn" logo. ZOO, a group of nine Japanese dancers, some with dreadlocks and all with deep tans, has caught on here, and itself influences fashion. The group sings lines like "I know you got soul!" but sticks to the stylish, marketable parts of street culture, forswearing all mention of inner-city violence, for instance. With its decidedly sunny disposition, ZOO recently recorded a video promotion in Hawaii.

But then there is Kozo Suzuki, who makes his living as a dancer at Tokyo Disneyland. He wants to make his own, peculiarly Japanese fashion statements. He does wear a baseball cap, but his reads: "Proud to Be Yellow."

— YUMIKO ONO

November 23, 1992

* * *

In Japan, Death on the Green Is Par for the Course

EDITOR'S NOTE: In one old golf joke, a man laments that his wife has threatened to leave him if he doesn't give up the game. It's too bad, he says. He'll miss her. The Japanese seem to have their own version of the joke, but it isn't a wife, it's a doctor who makes the threat, and the threat isn't divorce, it's death. Yes, the Japanese take golf seriously. It's a matter of honor to do things right—even when one is supposedly having fun.

TOKYO—An exhausted Takahiro Kawakita, arms splayed, slumps in a chair at the Ishihara Hills Golf Club. The middle-aged photo-company employee doesn't seem to notice the television set blaring in the corner, or the grasshopper sniffing his sweat-soaked handkerchief crumpled on the table before him. He is girding himself for the battle ahead.

"I don't have much time to talk," says the red-faced duffer, worn out from the morning's nine holes of golf. "I've got to be back on the course at 12:47."

Mr. Kawakita's sapped state is par for the course in Japan, where the Ministry of Health and Welfare has disclosed a terrible secret: In this country, golf kills.

> *"I've got a personal list of 64 people who died on the putting greens," says Keizo Kogure, sports doctor and author of "How to Die Early by Playing Golf."*

Golf is eight times more likely than running is to kill a Japanese man over 60, according to a ministry study. It is worse than tennis, mountaineering and croquet (which ranked surprisingly high).

"I've got a personal list of 64 people who died on the putting greens," says Keizo Kogure, sports doctor and author of "How to Die Early by Playing Golf." He figures that every year, about 4,750 golfers take the fairway to heaven.

A look at the stressful style of Japanese *gorufu,* as golf is called here, suggests why the nation has so many golf corpses.

Japan has more than 1,900 courses, and all are packed. Ishihara Hills, a public club two hours from Tokyo, books players up to three months ahead. "There are still a few vacancies in August," says manager Takuji Matsuzaki. "Everything else is taken."

"Everything" means every minute. The manager, a one-time Honda factory supervisor, spaces his foursomes just seven minutes apart, and the pressure is on to keep the line moving no matter what. Production time is down to six minutes at some other clubs, where reservations are sometimes made six months in advance.

If you miss your tee-off time, you could wait three more months for an opening. Tokyo travel agent Gaijiro Yamaguchi regularly crawls out of bed at 4 o'clock for an early-morning game. "Most of the other cars on the road at that hour are golfers," he says.

Not crazy, says John Stapleton, a U.S. executive schooled in the Japanese way of golf. "It's honor. You've got a commitment, so you go in spite of anything." Once, he says, "rain was blowing in sheets, and the trees were bent sideways from the wind." His partners came for him anyway. He has since played in snow, fog and gloom of night.

Whatever the weather, players usually rush to get to the club early so they can relax before the morning's round with a scotch and water.

Then on to the course, where caddies, usually hard-bitten older women, and mandatory on the links here, set the tone with a pre-tee-off lecture.

"There's no etiquette out there anymore," snaps Ishihara Hills caddie Miss Sakai, who declines to give her first name. With a fierce dab at her makeup, she snarls through her dentures. "Players should be able to finish in two hours." Throughout the game, she hectors players to speed up, slow down, to stay in formation with players ahead and behind.

Stressful as this hard-driving caddie may be, players are often burdened by another worry—their partners.

Yoshimitsu Fukuda frets and sweats next to the ninth green at the Tokyo Country Club. He is playing golf with clients, and there is pressure to keep them happy.

"I feel like I ought to lose on purpose, but then there's a risk that they'll figure it out," the 51-year-old bag manufacturer says. He nervously twists an empty cigarette pack. Sand bursts from the bunker behind him. Then more sand.

'Really Enjoying It'

"I'd be grateful if they could get a good score," he says plaintively.

The golfer eventually emerges from the sand trap. "I'm struggling, but I'm really enjoying it," he says, and Mr. Fukuda, a fresh pack of smokes in his pocket, happily scurries for the clubhouse.

"You've only got 30 minutes for lunch," his caddie barks at his back. "Hurry up."

Like caddies, lunch is mandatory at the links around Tokyo, even if players finish the front nine at 10 a.m.

"Try this, it's delicious," says Tsujiyo Takahashi from his beer-drenched clubhouse table. He proffers an artery-clogging sprig of broccoli wrapped in fatty bacon, encased in onion shavings, then dipped in batter and deep-fried. His tablemates dig into thick curries, pork chunks and, perhaps in a nod to nutrition, tofu.

Mr. Kawakita pours another scotch and water and contemplates the game's mysteries. "Sand traps are the most dangerous," he says through a mist of tobacco smoke. "Your blood pressure races in a bunker shot, and you die walking onto the green. People think it's the putting that kills you."

Up before dawn, putting while it pours, drinks before noon, forced marches, leaden lunches, chain-smoking.

What else?

Gambling. Really complicated gambling. Halfway through his game, Mr. Kawakita knits his brow. He has nine concurrent bets on this round. Among them: a close-to-the-pin bet, a putting bet, a halfway-score bet, a total-score bet.

Another Cause for Alarm

The stress isn't the stakes. They are usually small. It's the honor that is at stake: his, the client's, the foursome's, his company's, his client's company's.

At this point, a glorious hole in one would seem a gambler's dream. But in gorufu, it is cause for more alarm. A hole in one obligates the golfer to buy expensive gifts for his fellow players, throw a drinking party and plant a commemorative tree near the tee to mark his "joy." So golfers struggle to hit the ball close to the hole—but not too close. (To ease the mind, players can buy nearly $5,000 in hole-in-one insurance before the game for about $100.)

Once the last putt is made, it is off to the clubhouse for more drinking. Then maybe a party and dinner in town. Then more drinking. "One time I got up at 4 a.m., and got home at one in the morning," recalls Mr. Stapleton, the American executive.

And so it is that sleep deprivation, booze and pressures on the course make gorufu a real Type-A aorta-popper for out-of-shape players. But try telling that to Mr. Kawakita, the duffer at Ishihara Hills. Beet-faced and breathless, he is running back to the course for more relaxation.

"This is great," he exclaims, turning his head nervously as the clock ticks toward 12:46. "I've got a day off work!"

— QUENTIN HARDY

June 17, 1993

*   *   *

Voice of Democracy Bellows Loud and Clear in the Streets of Japan

EDITOR'S NOTE: In Japan, form extends even to political campaigning. Correct form is especially important to the "bush warbler," the woman who trumpets the candidate's name thousands of times a day over the loudspeaker on his roving sound truck. Everything she does follows the most stylized of rituals, from the precise moment of the day she begins her screeching to the way she accents certain syllables in the candidate's name. And the candidate? Often he goes along for the ride, shaking an occasional hand and trying to avoid being spotted catnapping by the voters.

TOKYO—As the sound truck rolls into the sleeping city neighborhood, a sudden bellow blasts away the morning calm.

"Hello everyone! Hello everyone! The humble Midori Ota! Midori Ota! Vote for Midori Ota!" booms the voice. Bedside clocks read 8:03 a.m. "We beg for your support! Ota! Ota! Midori Ota!"

> *The crucial thing for a politician is to make people remember his name. This leads to a lot of repetition, repetition, repetition from the trucks.*

In Japan, it is time to plug your ears, tape the windows and chain the dog. Hundreds of vans, trucks and passenger cars, each mounted with huge loudspeakers, are roving the land in praise of one or another of the 955 candidates for the July 18 national election.

Intrusive? Obstreperous? You bet. If one of the big machines passes your house, it practically peels the paint. Japan's political turmoil has brought out more candidates than usual for this election, and that means more sound trucks. Low-budget candidates are penetrating narrow alleys on sound bicycles, and sound barges ply Tokyo's canals.

The racket from Japan's well-amplified candidates is all too much for Susumu Ogura, who stands outside Kichijoji Station holding a sign advertising a karaoke hall. Halfway through his shift, he has already endured high-decibel pleas from a dozen speakers. "If you're just passing through, you can stand it," he says, grimacing, "but think what it's like for me. They've only been talking for 45 minutes and my ears are ringing."

For the Japanese politician, there isn't much alternative to using a sound truck. In the interest of fairness, candidates for the Diet are severely restricted in the number of television, radio and newspaper advertisements they may run. Door-to-door canvassing is forbidden. Posters and fliers are permitted, though, as are the sound trucks, and there's no cap on the clamor.

The crucial thing for a politician is to make people remember his name, since as many as a dozen candidates sometimes run in a single district. This leads to a lot of repetition, repetition, repetition from the trucks.

"I am Takashi Kosugi," thunders Takashi Kosugi, a 57-year-old Tokyo incumbent who has parked his sound van outside a busy railway station. "Takashi Kosugi, Takashi Kosugi. Tackling political reform with all his might is Kosugi. Takashi Kosugi. Takashi Kosugi." He repeats his message nonstop for half an hour, as hundreds of commuters hurry past.

"I need to promote my personality," Mr. Kosugi says later in an interview over a breakfast of a hamburger and french fries.

Some trucks produce more shrieking than speaking. The point is to project sincerity, and in Japanese politics, few things are more sincere than putting your—or a surrogate's—all into a shout. Playing a taped message, though not officially banned, is considered cheating.

"I really killed my voice, and I'm just getting started," says Masashi Saito, warm-up announcer for independent candidate Atsushi Yamamoto. Then he smiles. "Maybe if my voice gets really hoarse, we'll get the sympathy vote."

Candidate Yamamoto's staff also makes the rounds atop bicycles mounted with large bullhorns, front and rear. "We're reaching everyone with these," says one worker, patting his bike's bright red frame.

The Group of Seven summit in Tokyo last week encouraged extremists to turn up the political dissonance. Hiroyoshi Fudeyasu, head of a rightist group, adjusts his rising-sun headband. Since his group isn't a registered party, he says, "we're not allowed to make any political statements during elections." He raises his bullhorn. "So today we're having a religious service."

His "church" is Tokyo's busiest shopping area during a weekday lunch hour. He "prays" that the G-7 withhold aid to Russia. (To no avail: Russia was given $3 billion in help.) His bullhorn, according to its maker, has a 0.8-kilometer range.

All this in a culture that values peace and quiet. Blame the nation's aural hex on its political history. In the first national elections, held in 1890, just 1.1% of the population was eligible to vote. The right guy could get elected by making a few personal visits around the post-feudal domain. By 1925, though, eligible voters made up 20.1% of the population. Women's suffrage in 1945 turned all the adults into potential voters, but because of the campaigning restrictions, the need to relate personally to each voter remained.

"We got sound trucks about the same time we got automobiles," early in the century, says Ikuo Kabashima, professor of politics at Tsukuba University.

Japanese law usually prohibits any din of more than 85

decibels, slightly quieter than an elevated train roaring by. But when politicians made that law, they exempted themselves: During election campaigns, sound trucks can crank it up.

Voters enjoy the hubbub, Mr. Kosugi, the candidate for parliament, argues. "The Japanese like to feel close to the candidate," he says. Indeed, during a morning cruise through his constituency, one apron-clad woman does rush out to greet Mr. Kosugi's truck. But several commuters also snarl at Mr. Kosugi's fearsome speakers.

"Bush warblers" are supposed to ease the pain. These women, mostly in their 20s and hired from "narration-model" agencies, ride in the trucks to shout out the candidate's name. They are valued for having the honeyed, high-pitched female voices that many Japanese love.

"If the voice is too low, it doesn't travel far enough," says Takako Iwabuchi, a 15-year warbling veteran for Mr. Kosugi. "I raise mine at least one octave higher: 'This is TA-kashi KO-sugi,'" she sings, waving her index finger like a conductor's baton.

Inside the van, the warblers watch like hawks for shy supporters waving from their apartments. The voters must be answered by immediate loud-spoken thanks. When the truck blocks the road, Mr. Kosugi himself thunders an apology to the inconvenienced drivers—and reminds them of his name.

A pitch for every predicament. The truck turns into a placid, tree-lined lane. "We are bothering you residents of this quiet neighborhood," the speaker screeches to the surprised denizens. "Please excuse us because it is campaigning time. TA-kashi KO-sugi. TA-kashi KO-sugi. Please vote for TA-kashi KO-sugi."

— QUENTIN HARDY and YUMIKO ONO

July 14, 1993

SECTION FOUR

CREATIVITY, JAPANESE STYLE

Introduction

"We are a poor island nation with no natural resources."

"It is only a small gift, really nothing, but . . . "

"Alas, we Japanese are not creative."

When Japanese start to belittle themselves, wise foreigners raise their guard. It's not that the self-effacement is always a calculated lie. Sometimes—as with the natural resources—it's an expression of real, if misguided or exaggerated, insecurities. Sometimes—as with the gift—it's a mere reflex, the mark of a deep-rooted cultural preference for modesty.

Whatever the reason, the handwringing is often misleading. Even when the Japanese have real cause for concern, you can be sure they are working hard to compensate for the self-perceived handicap. They may have already overcome the difficulty without realizing it.

So it is with Japan's "creativity" deficiency. It is natural, perhaps, for a country that has borrowed so much know-how from other countries to worry that mimicry is its only talent. But borrowing heavily from abroad is natural for an industrializing country. The United States was considered an industrial "copycat" nation well into the 20th century. Its Nobel Prizes have mostly come in the last few decades.

And Nobel Prizes are by no means perfectly synonymous with creativity. Today we think of the creative person as a revolutionary who casts aside a previous order of things and defines new rules. That is too limited an understanding of creativity. Mozart obediently accepted and followed the rigid musical formats he inherited, from the sonata to the symphony to the mass. Yet he was surely one of history's most creative composers.

In similar fashion the Japanese *kaizen* system, with its accumulation of tiny improvements on well-established processes, is a form of creativity. Indeed, the best way to think of creativity may be as a spectrum or continuum. On one end is outright mimicry. On the other are gigantic perceptual leaps. Societies progress along the continuum as they develop, starting with mimicry and building toward the leaps.

A society that has produced the transistor radio, the Walkman and the bullet train has come a long way on the continuum. A society that has produced Godzilla, karaoke and the capsule hotel has the potential to achieve a strange but wonderful sort of creative greatness. The stories in this section explore the creative genius of a society that still tends to think of itself as not very creative.

* * *

Crawl In and Stay for the Night, Japanese Inn Beckons

EDITOR'S NOTE: Small cars. Small houses. Bonsai. Miniaturization comes naturally to a landscarce people. But carried to its logical extremes, the urge to miniaturize can produce startling results. Who but the Japanese would come up with the world's smallest hotel room, a cross between a washing machine and a coffin? Who but the Japanese would want to stay in such a room?

OSAKA—Still another example of Japanese inventiveness: a hotel room so cramped that you have to crawl into it.

Literally.

Scan the interior of the establishment that introduced the idea here in Japan's second-largest city. It looks more like a Laundromat than a place to spend the night. But what appear at first to be washers or dryers, stacked two-high in long rows along the dimly lit corridors, turn out to be sleeping "capsules."

The Capsule Inn Osaka, which calls itself a "business hotel for the year 2100," has 418 capsules spread over three floors of a nondescript downtown building. Each plastic capsule is four feet, 11 inches high; four feet, 11 inches wide; and six feet, seven inches deep.

> *About 30% of the guests on any given night are Osaka residents who missed the last train home after a night of carousing. The capsules are cheaper than cabs.*

Almost every night, almost every capsule is full. And people pay to stay there.

They don't pay much, which is the secret of the two-year-old inn's success. Real-estate costs here are among the world's highest, but the Capsule Inn's berthing space is squeezed into an area only one-third to one-fourth that of even its smallest competitors.

Only $11 a Night

So a night at the Capsule Inn costs the equivalent of only $11 ($2 extra for guests who want to use the elaborate sauna in the building's basement). That compares with $20 to $30 a night at the local "business hotels" that Japanese traveling salesmen normally patronize, and $75 to $100 a night at the Japanese hotels that American business travelers are accustomed to.

"I have only one purpose in coming here—to save money," says a 34-year-old salesman from Tokyo. A frequent guest, he once spent three straight nights in a Capsule Inn capsule.

Hidetoshi Yano, the crew-cut man with Yves St. Laurent cuff links who manages the Capsule Inn, explains it this way: The businessmen (women aren't allowed) who stay at the inn are on fixed daily expense accounts of $25 to $50, so "the less they spend on hotels, the more they can spend on eating, drinking and other things."

There are other attractions. Each capsule has a television set, radio, alarm clock, mirror and air conditioning. Television, vending machines and comfortable sofas are available in the lobby on each floor, where guests lounge in terry-cloth robes supplied by the management. (They're waiting in the locker where you check your suitcase and hang your clothes.) And then there is the sauna, one of a chain of five owned by Yukio Nakano, who also owns the inn.

Designed by Kisho Kurokawa, one of Japan's noted architects, the capsules have a futuristic appearance that appeals to some. A retired sailor is a regular guest. The capsules remind him of his shipboard berths. About 30% of the guests on any given night are Osaka residents who missed the last train home after a night of carousing. The capsules are cheaper than cabs.

Masami Kawanishi, a 35-year-old salesman for Kawasaki Heavy Industries who works in Osaka and lives 50 minutes away in Kobe, comes to the Capsule Inn once a month for another reason. "I like to get away from my wife and kids, use the sauna and read a book," Mr. Kawanishi says. He tells his wife he is working late. "She knows I'm coming here," he says. "She just doesn't know how early."

Mr. Kawanishi doesn't mind being confined to a capsule. He says it helps him concentrate on his reading. Other guests feel differently, though. Susumu Kaburaki, a 32-year-old computer installer for Hitachi Ltd., says that his first night in a capsule will be his last. "In view of the space, I don't think this place is so cheap," he says. "I won't come back even if I have to pay more elsewhere."

Stars and Meteorites
Mark Schreiber, reviewing the inn in the Tokyo Weekender, writes: "I'd give this Pillbox Hilton four stars for cleanliness, three stars for efficiency and one meteorite for comfort."

Forewarned by Mr. Schreiber, a colleague and I who recently spent a night at the Capsule Inn fortified ourselves at a local pub first and slept reasonably well. But not everyone comes with forewarning. "When they come here at first, many of our guests expect some sort of room," says Mr. Yano.

Mr. Yano also concedes that the fire department was less than thrilled with the Capsule Inn's building plans, and that the inn after two years of operation "isn't losing money but isn't making any big profit either." Still, he is convinced that capsules are the wave of the future.

Already two competing capsule establishments are operating, one here in Osaka and one in Nagoya. Another capsule hostelry, this one catering only to women, opened recently in Tokyo.

Mr. Yano thinks that capsule inns would be ideal for ski resorts and could even spread beyond Japan. "They provide all the necessary things—radio, TV, sleep," he says. "If similar inns were built in the U.S., I feel they would be quite popular."

— URBAN C. LEHNER

March 4, 1981

Editor's note: Suffice it to say that despite the optimistic note on which this story ends, capsule inns have not exactly swept the world. But they have swept Japan. While no one keeps exact figures, there are dozens in Tokyo alone.

Gaman, Japan's Brand of Stoicism, Adds Spice to Nation's TV Fare

EDITOR'S NOTE: A foreign visitor who turns on television in his Tokyo hotel room may be surprised to behold a quiz-show contestant tackling a squealing boar to see how long he can lie in bed with it. Endurance is highly prized in Japan, and one indicator of Japanese inventiveness is the national obsession with new and unusual endurance contests. They're standard TV fare today, but their origins are in the 19th century. Could this be what Oscar Wilde had in mind when he wrote, in 1891, "In fact, the whole of Japan is a pure invention."

TOKYO—Five men belly up to the counter at Hell Ramen Hyottoko, a restaurant decorated with images of devils.

As TV cameras whir, Morihiro Yamashita, a 28-year-old boxer, begins slurping a bowl of very spicy noodles, and soon his face is dripping with sweat. Mr. Yamashita gags as he bites into a piece of sushi that has been loaded up with a thick wad of green wasabi horseradish. (Normally, just a smidgen of that can bring tears to the eyes.) Finally, he digs into curried rice that has 120 times the usual spice. Poor Mr. Yamashita slaps himself on the face and tears off his pants.

Don't touch that dial: You're watching "TV Champion," a popular weekly Japanese game show. Mr. Yamashita was never a champ in the ring, but in this test of endurance, he bested his closest rival by three spoonfuls of curry to become Japan's Super-Spiciness King.

"I felt faint during the sushi," recalls Mr. Yamashita. In the curry round, he briefly lost his eyesight. "Halfway through, my tongue went numb," Mr. Yamashita says.

> *"TV Champion" is but one of a number of Japanese shows in which contestants vie for modest prizes and national attention by making heroic displays of* gaman, *endurance, long a cherished virtue in this hard-working nation.*

"TV Champion" is but one of a number of Japanese shows in which contestants vie for modest prizes and national attention by making heroic displays of *gaman,* endurance, long a cherished virtue in this hard-working nation. In a society that demands conformity, the programs also give ordinary people a chance to stand out from the crowd.

"For Japanese, this may be the easiest kind of TV program to enjoy," says social psychologist Hiroyoshi Ishikawa of Seijo University in Tokyo. Gaman tests have been popular since the 19th century, he notes, well before the advent of television. "In the summer, you'd shut yourself in a room, wear lots of clothes, turn on some heat and see how long you could stand it," says Prof. Ishikawa.

The tradition continues in modified form with the annual "Trans-America Ultra Quiz," which has become a national institution since it was first televised 17 years ago. Contestants travel from Tokyo to New York, taking trivia tests at about a dozen tourist spots along the way; one mistake too many, and a player is hustled onto the first flight back to Japan.

The latest installment, taped over a period of weeks last summer, began in a Tokyo stadium, where 26,121 players fielded true-false questions. The group of 55 who survived the preliminaries got to board a plane for Guam. Further winnowing took place in Hawaii, San Francisco and Valley Forge, Pennsylvania, before a final one-on-one on a yacht off Manhattan.

In Hawaii, the players were rousted out of bed at 2 a.m. for a pop quiz that dragged on almost till dawn. "I stayed up all night three times during the 10 days I was in the contest," says Hisanori Nogami, a 41-year-old financial analyst for IBM Japan Ltd. Like other losers, Mr. Nogami had to play a "punishment game" for the TV cameras after he was eliminated. His humiliation: painting a line down an airstrip more than a kilometer long, on a sunny, 38-degree-Celsius afternoon.

"Ultra Quiz" is entirely in character for a land where eight-year-olds cram for entrance exams and wear shorts to school in winter. "You've got to have the attitude that you absolutely won't lose," reflects reigning 22-year-old champ Kenichi Tanaka, a junior at Tokyo University. "No matter what, if you don't have strong will, you can't do it."

The players fielded such questions as: "How do you say 'USTR' (U.S. Trade Representative) in Japanese?" To prepare, Mr. Tanaka says, he subscribed to three Japanese newspapers and 10 magazines, "because 'Ultra Quiz' has lots of current-affairs questions." He also belongs to his college's Quiz Research Committee, 70 students who meet four hours each Saturday to drill one another with trivia questions.

Masato Ikui tackled a squealing boar and lay in bed with it on a December episode of "Live, Live, Live, Live Downtown," a dating show. He went on to win a date and a million yen ($8,300) in prize money, but Mr. Ikui says he wasn't in it for the cash.

"I like to express myself," explains the 42-year-old caterer. "Most people go to work, go home, maybe play golf. I like to expose everything that's inside me."

Some participants seek exposure of a different sort.

Consider "*Shiroi Koibito* Battle Royal in the Snow," a late-January special that was shot on the frigid northern island of Hokkaido. A show hostess rolls a huge foam ball down an incline at 10 college students dressed as bowling pins, knocking nine to the snow. She flattens the 10th for the spare.

Gaman spectacles, of course, aren't unique to Japan. The U.S., for example, has progressed from goldfish-swallowing and phone-booth-packing to mud-wrestling and the TV show "American Gladiators," reported to be a favorite of President Bill Clinton.

Although the Japanese shows may offer a glimpse into the national psyche, they aren't for everyone. Indeed, some Japanese contend gaman is passé, especially among the spoiled younger generation.

But try telling that to Naonori Tsunoda, who suffered internal bleeding after placing third in the spicy-food contest. "I'm the kind of person who likes to challenge himself to the limit," says the 28-year-old record-company employee. In college, Mr. Tsunoda says he placed eighth in a 30-man gaman meet in which he was lashed to a wheel and rolled through a pond. "It's a little sadistic, isn't it?" he says.

Even macho men have their off days. In last Thursday night's "TV Champion" broadcast, boxer Mr. Yamashita lost the Super-Spiciness King title in his first defense. "I had a hangover," he explains.

Furthermore, to capture the essence of gaman, programs sometimes cheat a bit.

In "TV Champion's Foreigner Japan-Expert Contest,"

which ran early last year, 30-year-old Philip Silverstein and several other foreign men fielded trivia questions in Japanese. But before responding, each had to gobble such Japanese delicacies as a bowl of live *shirouo,* matchstick-sized squiggling fish.

Mr. Silverstein and two opponents were later expected to answer the final round of questions while sitting in the painful *seiza* meditation position—bare feet tucked under rump, back ramrod-straight. One of the hosts had the camera zoom in on the feet. "Look, they're blue!" he observed, jabbing his finger into their soles. Andy Smith, a 24-year-old American, won the title after acing questions about sumo wrestling and Japanese culture.

Trouble is, much of the contest was faked. Mr. Silverstein says the contestants were supplied by a talent agency, and he was paid 15,000 yen a day for four days of taping. The show's staff fed some questions and answers to players in advance, he says.

Yoshiharu Inukai, the show's producer, says "TV Champion" had to use an agency because the episode was filmed before the series had its broadcast debut last spring, so there was no way to enlist players from among the viewing audience, as the show started doing once it got off the ground. "We input a certain degree of Japan-related information to the five finalists beforehand," he concedes, "and also told them some of the quiz answers."

Still, the Japan-expert contest wasn't totally rigged. "Those were real blue feet," says Mr. Silverstein. "I remember limping to the train station after it was over."

— MICHAEL WILLIAMS

March 8, 1993

* * *

It's Time to Talk Turkey About Japanese Turkeys

EDITOR'S NOTE: Monkey see, monkey do. That's the rap on the Japanese. Slavish imitators. Uncreative. Well, maybe. No question, the Japanese have proved themselves adept mimics. But that's not the whole story. For every Japanese patisserie chef who makes his croissants precisely the way he was taught to in Paris, there's a Yutaka Goto, who takes a Western dish like turkey and prepares it in a distinctly Japanese fashion.

SHIHORO—And now, in the spirit of Thanksgiving, it's time to talk a little turkey about Japanese turkeys.

No, senator. By "turkeys," we don't mean those conniving Japanese bureaucrats who throw up such clever barriers to foreign products entering Japan. We're talking about the genuine article, what the Japanese call *shichimencho,* the bird of seven faces.

On this most American of holidays, Americans among our readers may be thankful to know that we have investigated the situation at length and have determined to a certainty that American consumers won't soon be flocking to Japanese turkeys the way they flocked to Japanese cars and cameras. Some things are sacred.

Starch Factory

Our method of inquiry was to pay a visit to this town of 7,000 on Hokkaido, Japan's northernmost island. Shihoro, the center of a potato- and beet-growing area, is about 25 kilometers by car from Obihiro, which is about 220 kilometers by train from Sapporo, which is 865 kilometers by air from Tokyo. It

boasts Asia's largest starch factory, a boast believable by anyone who has breathed the air for miles downwind. It also
boasts one Yutaka Goto, who in Japan is to turkeys what the
first steak-restaurant owner in India was to cows.

> *The city of Shihoro also boasts one*
> *Yutaka Goto, who in Japan is to tur-*
> *keys what the first steak-restaurant*
> *owner in India was to cows.*

Like his father before him, Mr. Goto, a youthful-looking
50-year-old, runs a small *ryokan,* Japanese-style inn, called
Kikuya (literally Chrysanthemum Place) a couple blocks from
Shihoro's railroad station. Though named after a flower,
Kikuya features a decorational motif that is heavy on animals. In the foyer among other specimens are two stuffed elk
head, a stuffed otter, a stuffed pheasant, two deserted bees
nests and several cages of live parakeets. "I love animals,"
Mr. Goto repeats frequently in the course of a conversation
that stretches over several hours.

It was because he and his father loved animals that they
were originally entrusted with the turkeys. The first three birds
were originally the property of an officer in the World War II
Japanese army, who kept them as pets. Stationed in nearby
Obihiro when the war ended, he tried to set himself up in
Shihoro as a farmer. But, as Mr. Goto observes, "officers are
not trained to be farmers." When the officer's farm failed, he
gave the turkeys to his friends the Gotos.

No Turkey Tradition
Now to follow the plot from here you need to know a few
things about Japanese eating and cooking habits. First, there's

no tradition of eating turkey here. The bird isn't native to Japan (one dictionary on our shelf suggests it's native to, well, Turkey, but that somehow seems too pat). Then, too, says Yoshio Tabata, a culinary expert at Ajinomoto Co., a food-products maker, "We Japanese don't like the taste of turkey."

Actually, Mr. Tabata immediately corrects himself: "Most of us have never tried it." Despite considerable Westernization of the Japanese diet, rice remains the staple food, and in the cramped kitchens of Japan's cramped houses the electric rice cooker remains the main cooking utensil. Large ovens are relatively rare. And no one in Japan has yet invented a subcompact turkey. You get the picture.

But in the poverty-stricken years right after the war, food was often scarce. So love animals though they did, the Gotos began serving turkey meat to guests at the Kikuya. And how would you serve turkey to a people with the aforementioned dietary habits, to a people whose favorite food after rice is raw fish?

"We Japanese," explains Mr. Goto's younger brother Yasuhiro, who recently opened a Kikuya restaurant in Sapporo, "like everything raw."

That they do. Starting with the ubiquitous sushi bars, which feature raw-fish dishes, restaurants specializing in raw horse, raw beef, raw chicken and raw game can be found in various parts of the country. But as for turkey, the Gotos claim that they alone in all Japan serve shichimen *ryori,* meaning "turkey cuisine, Japanese style."

Sitting on the straw-mat floors of the serving rooms at the Kikuya in Shihoro or on stools at the cypress-wood bar of the Kikuya in Sapporo, the turkey lover may partake of slices of raw turkey-breast meat made up to look like rose petals. This "turkey sashimi" is frozen as soon as the bird is butchered to ward off germs, and it's eaten like regular sashimi, dipped in soy sauce. Kikuya's patrons may also order turkey sukiyaki or turkey *nabe,* two traditional Japanese stewlike dishes that can be cooked with any meat, turkey *yakitori,* charcoal-grilled on skewers—even smoked turkey "ham" or "bacon." About all they can't get is roast turkey and dressing.

But that doesn't seem to hurt business. Mr. Goto in Shihoro keeps 300 turkeys on hand at a time and another 400 in the freezer. He and his six employees (including his wife and daughter) serve as many as 80 guests a night; once they've tasted raw turkey, Japanese like Osamu Kawamoto, a 31-year-old regular customer of the Kikuya in Sapporo, often pay it the ultimate compliment the Japanese, with their distinctive tastes, pay food: It's *sappari shita,* which means plain.

As a result business in Shihoro is so good that Mr. Goto has become "pretty selective" about accepting guests for the night; it's more profitable, he says, to run a restaurant than an inn. Government bureaucrats in charge of promoting small business often point to the Kikuyas as an unusual success story, Mr. Goto says, and the Kikuya and its turkeys have been the subject of numerous Japanese television features.

But Mr. Goto has no ambition to turn Japan on to turkey by opening branches in other parts of the country. His existing business is so profitable that he's attracting unfavorable attention at the tax collector's office, so there's no point in expanding, he says.

Others think that even were Mr. Goto inclined to expand, his potential as a purveyor of raw turkey would be limited. Lack of ovens is the real problem with promoting turkeys in Japan, says Hideyuki Kojima, whose Nishifu Turkey Farm in Fuchu, about 30 kilometers west of Tokyo, produces the lion's share of Japan's annual output of 60,000 turkeys. "Many Japanese households," says Mr. Kojima, "lack the means to eat turkey that tastes good." (His output goes mainly to hotels, which roast it Western style.)

Actually, other Japanese entrepreneurs have tried to imitate the Gotos, but Mr. Goto says all have failed. The reason, he says, is that they didn't love animals. Mr. Goto can't explain why, but this much he knows: "It's impossible to succeed in this business if you don't love animals."

— URBAN C. LEHNER

November 24, 1982

*   *   *

Godzilla No. 18 Wreaks Havoc on Tokyo's City Hall

EDITOR'S NOTE: Horror-film fans have known it since the 1950s: The Japanese are creative. Toho Co. and other Japanese movie makers have devised demons and monsters that surprise foreigners and Japanese alike with their originality. The most famous of these is Gojira, an outsized half-gorilla, half-whale. Westerners know Gojira as Godzilla. The 18th Godzilla movie, "Godzilla vs. King Ghidora," never played in American theaters, but did well enough in Japan that Toho has released a number of sequels, including "Godzilla vs. Space Godzilla" and "Godzilla vs. Destroyer."

TOKYO—How does a movie series about a rampaging mutant dinosaur keep going strong after its 16th sequel? What's the appeal of a 100-meter behemoth who can't walk through a town without smashing it up?

"He destroys famous buildings," explains Hidekichi

Yamane, who is Godzilla's publicity man at Toho Co., Japan's biggest domestic movie maker, and since 1954 the studio that has brought the world tales of Godzilla, the King of Monsters. "Human beings want to destroy tall buildings, but they can't. Godzilla can destroy them easily."

The films have something to say about human nature, and about living vicariously through lizards.

> *"I feel relieved when he destroys buildings. It's as if Godzilla is destroying the city full of gaudiness,"* *says Mr. Omori, who has directed the three most recent Godzillas.*

In his soon-to-be released No. 18, "Godzilla vs. King Ghidora," Godzilla is, as usual, a very "now" reptile. The Sultan of Saurians levels Tokyo's new 160-billion-yen ($1.22 billion) city hall, a 48-story marble-and-steel complex that for many Tokyoites symbolizes the excesses of Japan in the late '80s.

But that's only after he kills the Americans.

Toho is confident the Lizard King will recoup its 1.5-billion-yen investment in "King Ghidora" when Godzilla is once more unleashed on Japan in December. Godzilla has sold 73 million tickets locally over the past 37 years. It has played in more than 50 countries. The latest Godzilla vehicle will probably make it to the U.S. by mid-1992.

In Japan, he is known as Gojira, an amalgam of gorilla and *kujira,* the word for whale. And his secret of success is in keeping up with the times. When he was first starting out, he merely terrorized townspeople. Godzilla today seems to have a social conscience—attacking environmental pollution, energy dependence and genetic engineering. In the process, he has won millions of Japanese fans—and a small fan club, called Godzilla Freaks Clan. Some like him for what he does to cities with his blue death-ray, and some, appreciating subtext, like Godzilla as a guardian of Japan's deeper feelings.

"I've gone to Godzilla movies every New Year season since I was born," says Haruhiko Okiyama, a 27-year-old freelance interior designer. "He is the symbol of justice."

In "King Ghidora," the monster for all seasons stays up-to-date by playing to Japan's continuing obsession with World War II and its irritation with growing pressure from abroad to open its markets.

The plot: People from the 23rd century (mostly white males who occasionally speak in exaggerated American accents) go to a Pacific island in 1944, where Godzilla saves Japanese troops under siege by Americans. Godzilla kills the U.S. soldiers but is hauled off to the Bering Sea by the time travelers.

The Future Folk unleash on modern Japan King Ghidora, a three-headed dragon. Emi, Japanese heroine of the future, defects from the ranks of the Caucasians and discloses their fiendish mission: to force Japan to buy foreign computers and deny the country its economic destiny.

There's a big fight. Not to give away too much, but Godzilla is very much alive at the end of the picture. Somebody else isn't. Tokyo's governor needs new offices.

According to Kazuki Omori, the film's writer-director, the destruction of city hall expresses Japanese ambivalence about prosperity. "I feel relieved when he destroys buildings. It's as if Godzilla is destroying the city full of gaudiness," says Mr. Omori, who has directed the three most recent Godzillas.

Moviegoer Mr. Okiyama, who says he will be happy to spend 1,700 yen ($13) on a ticket to see Godzilla fight city hall, takes a more extreme personal view: "I can't stand it that he's smaller than the Tokyo metropolitan government. I want him to destroy it all."

To inspire such partisanship, such fanatical devotion, Godzilla must be played with strength but sensitivity. That's where Kenpachiro Satsuma comes in. He has known Godzilla from the inside since 1985.

The 72-kilo actor in an 80-kilo lizard suit is a study in dedication. "I've never talked with other actors who played Godzilla; you have to learn it physically," says Mr. Satsuma, who had portrayed the Smog Monster earlier in his career. "Playing Godzilla is different from playing a normal monster. You have to figure out how to be violent and gentle."

Originally a fictional byproduct of U.S. hydrogen-bomb tests, the first Godzilla (the original Japan basher) destroyed the old Toho Studios headquarters on his 1954 maiden rampage. The movie sold 9.6 million tickets at home. For the film's U.S. release, Toho spliced in 20 minutes, of Raymond Burr mostly. It's a camp classic.

But "there is revenge at the bottom of the movie," says Yukio Akatsuka, a well-known social commentator. "Monsters born from a threat in real society have become more popular."

By 1963, Japan had largely recovered from the war materially, it was booming economically, and it had nuclear-power plants of its own. Accordingly, Godzilla, ever a social chameleon, turned soft on atomic energy and defended Japan against various scary beasts.

Japan's hard-won prosperity made audiences want to have fun at the movies, Mr. Yamane says, "so Godzilla started fighting other monsters." In his heyday, he fought one a year.

And he got to be adorable. "Frightening creatures become cute after you see them often," says Mr. Akatsuka.

Today, the Reigning Reptile brings Toho more than five billion yen a year in trinket sales. Products range from wine decanters to a battery-powered Godzilla toilet-paper dispenser that roars when it rolls.

By the mid-'70s, with monster possibilities pretty much played out, Toho worried that Godzilla's tale was dragon on too long and tried to retire the Hoary Gila. But popular demand brought him back. Godzilla was a family favorite. As Mr. Yamane, Godzilla's PR man, puts it: Godzilla "makes for good communication between fathers and sons."

His comeback movie "Godzilla 1985" reunited Himself with his old nemesis Mr. Burr, who plays a United Nations official.

The comeback flick played in 1,500 U.S. theaters, according to Mr. Yamane. "That's a big booking for a Japanese movie." The acclaimed films of Akira Kurosawa, on the other hand, more commonly "play in five or six theaters," he notes.

Given its anti-American overtones, the 1991 Godzilla may not be boffo at the U.S. box office. But Toho still expects to find an American distributor.

Die-hard fan Mr. Okiyama doesn't foresee any problem, either. "My American friends say Godzilla is the only Japanese star that would make it in Hollywood. I agree. When Americans talk about him, their eyes become like children's."

If the Saber-Toothed Salamander keeps filling theaters, Toho plans to make its new-look Godzilla movies every two or three years. As 23rd-century Emi says, "Of course, I'll come back. I really like this era."

But Mr. Satsuma, the man in the belly of the beast, will need better ventilation in his lizard costume if he is to appear in a fourth Godzilla movie. The suit he wears has just a dozen tiny air holes around the neckline. Sometimes it gets hard to breathe when he takes out a skyscraper.

— QUENTIN HARDY

October 28, 1991

At Weddings in Japan, the Guests May Be Rented

EDITOR'S NOTE: Sometimes the key to creativity lies in seeing the obvious. Let's say your problem is you don't have any friends to attend your wedding. An uncreative person might just accept his fate and have the wedding with a short guest list. A creative person will see immediately that the solution is to go out and hire some shills to attend the wedding pretending they're friends. And a truly creative person will start a business renting shills for such occasions.

TOKYO—A Japanese wedding reception would be an utter failure without executives, bureaucrats and, of course, dear friends in attendance. So what is a groom to do when he doesn't know any important businessmen or government officials—and his bride doesn't have any friends?

One possibility is to rent guests, appearances being more important than reality. For between 15,000 yen ($180) and 50,000 yen per person, a little Tokyo company called Neko-No-Te provides plausible stand-ins for anything from weddings to openings, even funerals.

Takeo Miyashita last year played the part of an executive of a bride's company when she married a Tokyo policeman. At the reception in a downtown hotel, Mr. Miyashita gave a speech full of platitudes about the good job the bride was doing at the office. The groom knew it was a sham, but neither his parents nor his new in-laws figured it out. Nor, it seems, did the 80 policemen present. They were real but credulous.

Neko-No-Te provides people for about one wedding a month. Its biggest job so far was a wedding last year for which it provided 60 of the bride's 80 guests.

> ## *Clients rent ringers for various reasons, one of which is to tone up a guest list.*

Clients rent ringers for various reasons, one of which is to tone up a guest list. Because working for the government has cachet in Japan, even anonymous bureaucrats make desirable wedding guests. Childhood classmates are essential for showing how well-rounded the happy couple are. And company officials are like members of the extended family, given that a job here can last a lifetime.

Guest rental also can be a way to save money: It sometimes is cheaper to hire someone to portray Aunt Sumiko from the hinterland than it is to foot her train fare and a hotel bill.

Then too, invited guests sometimes can't come. "We get the seating chart with a gap where an official from Nikko Securities was supposed to sit," says Hideto Katamine, the founder of Neko-No-Te. "Then we have to find someone who knows at least a little about Wall Street, just in case the guy in the next seat talks to him."

The pretense works, partly because ceremonies in Japan are so formalized. Wedding receptions are very elegant, but guests don't mingle. They sit in their assigned seats, listening to pro forma speeches. There are no intimate asides, no effusion on the beauty of the bride, no cracks about the mothers-in-law. Even the three-tiered wedding cakes with pink roses and figurines aren't all they seem: The piece the bride and groom slice is real; the rest is wax and rented.

"The customers aren't trying to show off as much as they are creating the proper form," says Noboru Takeo, the president of an electrical-wire business who has made appearances as matchmaker, groom's best friend and bride's boss.

On one of his assignments, Mr. Takeo stood in for the father of the bride at a series of ritualized pre-wedding meetings with the in-laws-to-be. And he found himself in the middle of a soap opera: The father he was impersonating had deserted the family, but because the groom's father was a company president, the bride didn't want to put the nuptials in jeopardy. The bride and her mother wanted to cover up a shameful divorce until after the knot was tied. "I have no particular interest in drama," says Mr. Takeo. "They said they would explain my disappearance afterward."

Neko-No-Te's repertory company of 300 stand-ins are students, teachers, presidents of small companies, housewives. Many are friends, or friends of friends, of the company's staff. Like professional actors, they make an effort to get in character. If they are lucky, they get to meet the client before the gig. Usually, however, they make do with the single-page autobiographies clients fax to Neko-No-Te.

Neko-No-Te didn't get into business to rent bodies. It is one of several hundred Tokyo handyman businesses, called *benriya*. Neko-No-Te means The Cat's Paw, a reference to a Japanese saying about being so busy that you want even the cat to lend a hand. Most of its 40-million-yen revenue comes from house cleaning, deliveries and other odd jobs, but its shill business is substantial. The company's slogan: "If it's a job a human being can do . . . we'll take it on."

Neko-No-Te provides people for smaller affairs, too. It even has sent "close friends" to make up tennis doubles. But it plays by certain definite rules: Protect clients' privacy at all times, avoid jobs that smack of prostitution and don't do anything illegal.

Sometimes, however, the professional stand-ins tread rather close to the line. Mr. Takeo's wife was sent on a trip with a real-estate agent who was trying to sell resort properties to retired couples. Because Japanese prefer to travel in groups, Neko-No-Te stand-ins produced a group of shills to accompany bona fide customers.

Shills seem to like the work. After all, they get to eat and drink—and maybe even have fun. But some Japanese are put off by the stand-in business. Says a 31-year-old Tokyo office worker: "It makes me wonder whether I can even trust my own friends when they tell me who went to their wedding."

— ELISABETH RUBINFIEN

March 31, 1989

* * *

At Certain Clubs in Japan, the Singer May Be . . . You

EDITOR'S NOTE: People either love it or hate it, but everybody's heard of it. Far from a passing fad, karaoke is still all the rage in Japan, a decade and a half after its invention, even though other Japanese fads of the times—like partly nude coffee-shop hostesses—have disappeared. So widespread has it become outside Japan that some of its overseas devotees are unaware of its Japanese origins. But in the opportunity it provides for the individual to emerge from the all-smothering group, karaoke is still very much an answer to the needs of Japanese society.

GORA—Foreigners who have encountered Japanese tourists may think of the Japanese as quiet, self-effacing and shy. Those foreigners have never encountered karaoke.

> *A man who identifies himself only as Mr. Japanese Crazy Boy leans boozily into a microphone, peers at a song book and begins to wail.*

Saturday night in this mountain resort is a good place for such an encounter. The scene is a neighborhood *sunakku,* which in Japan isn't food and drink but a place to consume them. Patrons are seated on the straw-mat floor, all but one of them. At the counter with a scotch and water, a man who identifies himself only as Mr. Japanese Crazy Boy leans boozily into a microphone, peers at a song book and begins to wail a song about a jilted lover.

Crazy Boy and the blaring music that accompanies him can be heard up and down the block. When he finishes, the other patrons applaud, and soon one of them, equally tipsy, takes over the mike. Again the bar is suffused with crooning that, while hardly on key, most assuredly flows from the heart.

Good for the Heart

This is karaoke, and it is a craze that has swept Japan like few before it. From obscure origins a few years back, the fad of solo tavern singing to loud recorded accompaniment has attracted millions of fans and converted tens of thousands of nightclubs and sunakkus into karaoke bars. The lure of karaoke (pronounced kah-rah-o-kay, with no accent) is more or less as Crazy Boy explains his feelings: "Singing makes my heart feel good."

Others attempt deeper analyses for the phenomenon, having to do with a supposed longing to be free of Japanese society's binding traditions and its submersion of the individual in team efforts. "In karaoke, the spotlight is on the individual singer," one Japanese woman notes. "A lot of Japanese hunger for that kind of attention."

Spirituous beverages also seem to be a factor. It is often said that drunks are forgiven anything in Japan, that if during a drinking bout you tell off your boss or are otherwise indiscreet, all you need say the next morning is, "I was drunk."

To this mix, karaoke bars add the enticement of deafening background music. (The music, besides being loud, is always recorded; literally karaoke means "empty orchestra.") And as further encouragement to the timid, the microphone is turned up to provide echo-chamber reverberation. "Even if you aren't good, you can feel as if you have talent when you stand in front of the microphone," says Fumitoshi Nakamura, a 28-year-old dress-company salesman—and singer.

Anything goes in the selection of songs. But singers lean to what, in the American country-music idiom, might be called somebody-done-someone-wrong songs. Drowning one's sorrows in booze is a common theme, and one popular tune is entitled "Kanashii Sake," which means "sad sake."

But cheery numbers also are sung—whatever fits the singer's mood. The problem isn't the kind of song. "The problem," says a karaoke-bar owner in Tokyo, "is that the singers are either really good or really bad." Even more than for the bar owner, this is a problem for the people who live next door.

But suppose the urge to croon strikes when no tavern is near, when, say, one is in transit. No problem. Japan National Railways has lounge cars on a number of its trains that are equipped with a karaoke setup. And Setsuo Kato, a Tokyo cab driver, offers karaoke right in his taxi. "Nowadays, even single women sing in my cab," says Mr. Kato.

Or one can warble in the privacy of one's home. Although getting into the shower might seem simpler, more and more Japanese are purchasing home karaoke sets, consisting of a cassette player, a song book, tapes of background music, a microphone, an amplifier and speakers. Matsushita Electric Industrial Co., one of the main suppliers, says the market for all karaoke gear more than doubled last year to $18.2 million. It may hit $30 million this year.

Look Ma, No Pants

No segment of the populace is immune. Recently, police in Otsu arrested a Buddhist monk for selling a treasured wooden statue entrusted to his care and using the $2,300 in proceeds to buy a home karaoke set. The monk was freed when he bought the statue back—for $3,600.

Still, there are those who say karaoke has reached its peak. Matsushita doesn't expect sales of equipment to grow much after 1982. And now some Tokyo karaoke bars are converting to what may be the next Japanese fad, *no-pan kissa.* Kissa means tearoom. No-pan means no pants, and it refers to the kissas' hostesses. Actually, the hostesses do wear pants; it's just that they're very hard to see.

— URBAN C. LEHNER

July 14, 1981

* * *

Japan's Maverick Economist Keeps His Eye On the Sun

EDITOR'S NOTE: Someone once observed that intelligence recognizes what has happened, while genius recognizes what will happen. The creative genius is often a man like Yuji Shimanaka, who has very strong ideas, indeed, about what will happen. A man who, even in a conformist place like Japan, will quit his job rather than trim his sails. A man whose ideas are ever so slightly . . . how shall we say . . . unusual. So is Yuji Shimanaka a creative genius? Judge for yourself from the following story.

TOKYO—Yuji Shimanaka thinks he knows what's ailing the global economy. Sunspots.

Sunspots?

"All revolutionary theories take time to sink in," Mr. Shimanaka says. "This one is bigger than Keynesianism. It's broader than Marxism. It may be the most fundamental discovery since the general equilibrium theory of [Leon] Walras," an obscure 19th-century Frenchman whose work nevertheless has been called the Magna Carta of economics.

Magnum Opus

The 30-year-old economist's magnum opus is taking shape at a tiny metal desk squeezed between a file cabinet and wall lockers in a corner of the Japan Economic Research Center's offices here. Dozens of pieces of tape, with the corners of discarded charts and graphs trapped beneath them, dot a long-unpainted wall beside the desk.

On Mr. Shimanaka's desk lies a research paper filled with

graphs. Although the relationships in the graphs aren't always clear to the untrained eye, Mr. Shimanaka insists they provide evidence that solar activity affects the earth, human behavior and, ultimately, business cycles.

> *"This one is bigger than Keynesianism. It's broader than Marxism."*

Mr. Shimanaka says his graphs also indicate that war and peace, technological revolutions and economic swings track the waxing and waning of solar activity with uncanny consistency. When solar activity rises, he says, the earth grows warmer, crops grow more abundantly and commodity prices fall. When solar activity decreases, the climate grows harsher and inflation sets in.

Solar activity bottomed out most recently around 1976. So until the end of the century, Mr. Shimanaka says, most of the world can count on a lousy economy.

Many economists these days note similarities between the 1920s and the 1980s. Crumbling commodity prices, soaring stock markets, out-of-kilter world trade and lopsided capital balances contributed to the Great Depression, and all these problems are around again. A few Japanese economists even say a plunge in Tokyo stock prices could trigger the next global economic tailspin.

But probably no one has spun a doomsday scenario quite like that of Mr. Shimanaka. His sweeping vision takes in cosmic rays, magnetic activity and the human nervous system. In the past few months Mr. Shimanaka has propounded his theory in academic meetings, professional journals and a few minor general-interest magazines, a modest start for a theory he predicts will set the study of economics on its ear.

Although Mr. Shimanaka's presentations have been received cordially at such places as Bank of Japan's research center and Marubeni Corp., a trading company, not everyone has been swept away. "The statistical coincidences are interesting, but the cause-and-effect reasoning isn't terribly persuasive," says Hisao Kanamori, a Japanese economist. "Sunspots may be one tiny factor affecting human behavior, but there are so many other things."

'Food for Thought'

Mr. Kanamori, who also is president of the Japan Economic Research Center, happens to be Mr. Shimanaka's boss. But he isn't trying to dissuade Mr. Shimanaka from pursuing the theory. "It is food for thought," Mr. Kanamori willingly admits.

Mr. Shimanaka appreciates the research center's intellectual tolerance. Although he appears to be a typical company employee—with his suits, short hair and mild manner—there's an element of the maverick in him. He came to the research center after quitting a job in the economics department of a major bank. "I had ideas," he says, "and I didn't like to have them squelched."

Like most theories, Mr. Shimanaka's owes much to the earlier work of others. He has breathed new life into research done by a largely forgotten 19th-century British economist and chemist named William Stanley Jevons.

Jevons, pulling together the observations of Sir John Herschel, an astronomer, and Clement Juglar, a French business-cycle theoretician, concluded that sunspots indirectly determine business cycles. Herschel had found a correlation between sunspots and wheat prices, while Juglar had noted that the price of wheat had a trickle-down effect on the rest of the economy. But as the relative importance of wheat diminished, the Jevons thesis was largely written off.

Stunning Breakthrough

Some 110 years later, Mr. Shimanaka, browsing through bookstores in Tokyo's Kanda district, chanced upon the work of a Tokyo University astrophysicist named Hirokazu Yoshimura. For the past decade Mr. Yoshimura has been building a theory of 55-year grand solar cycles based on 11-year cycles recognized in earlier research.

Mr. Yoshimura's research, which has been published in the American Astronomical Society's journal, has yielded articles with titles such as "The Solar-Cycle Period-Amplitude Relation as Evidence of Hysteresis of the Solar-Cycle Nonlinear Magnetic Oscillation and the Long-Term (55-Year) Cyclic Modulation."

"I was stunned," Mr. Shimanaka says. Here was a breakthrough. Fifty-five years happened to be the span—give or take a few years—assigned by the Soviet economist Nikolai Kondratieff to his work on economic "waves," or long-term economic cycles. The Great Depression started just over 55 years ago, following the U.S. stock-market collapse in 1929.

Mr. Shimanaka telephoned Mr. Yoshimura to explain the possible economic implications of the professor's research. Mr. Yoshimura was bemused but interested.

"Some people hesitate to accept ideas that seem at first absurd," says Mr. Yoshimura, who has won a fellowship at the National Aeronautics and Space Administration's Marshall Flight Center in Alabama. "But in the 19th century some people thought the notion that the sun caused the aurora borealis was absurd. Eventually, it was proved."

Wide-Ranging Enquiry

"The sun influences cosmic rays, cosmic rays may influence weather, and weather may influence human behavior," he adds. "Cosmic rays are known to affect integrated circuits. So I cannot deny [Mr. Shimanaka's] theory."

Believing he had found in Mr. Yoshimura another Herschel, Mr. Shimanaka embarked on a wide-ranging enquiry into research on the sun and man. He came upon the work of Hiroshi Maeda of Kyoto University, who contended that solar activity affects magnetic activity, which affects hemoglobin density. "Hemoglobin condition certainly contributes to mass behavior," says Mr. Shimanaka, advancing the argument further.

Mr. Shimanaka also has incorporated the studies of Tadanobu Tsunoda, the doctor who wrote "The Japanese Brain." Mr. Tsunoda says human brains are swayed by the moon's cycles. And lunar cycles, Mr. Shimanaka notes, essentially are functions of the sun.

Sensing a grain of skepticism in an interviewer, Mr. Shimanaka bows his head slightly and grins. "People may find it all a little far-fetched at first," he says, "but I'm more and more confident that once others begin studying the theory, it will gain acceptance."

Besides, the graphs show the time is ripe for creative thinking. "Innovation rises when the economy declines," Mr. Shimanaka says. "And it's been exactly two Yoshimura cycles since Jevons."

— CHRISTOPHER J. CHIPELLO

September 1, 1986

Editor's note: Mr. Shimanaka, now a senior economist at Sanwa Research Institute, still believes in the sunspot theory, although he has mellowed somewhat and now relies on other indices as well in following the economy. Using his theory, he predicts the earth will become colder in the first half of the next century, leading to supply shortages and a period of inflation around 2030 similar to that experienced a few decades ago.

SECTION FIVE

INDIVIDUALISM, JAPANESE STYLE

Introduction

Japan stresses the group, the West (and America in particular) the individual. Stereotypes usually have some grounding in fact, and there's considerable grounding for this one.

An American may stay at the office late, but when his work is done he goes home. A Japanese who stays at the office late delays his departure until *everyone* is done working to avoid disrupting the harmony of the group.

Americans teach their children that "just because everyone else is doing it doesn't mean it's right." Japanese teach their children that "the nail that sticks out gets hammered down."

America's favorite rural metaphor is the cowboy, the lone individual on horseback. Japan's favorite rural metaphor is the rice-growing village, where farmers decide as a group on the appropriate water level.

All true enough, and yet a stereotype by definition is an oversimplification. A stereotype of a group emphasizes traits many members have in common and glosses over individual (there's that word again) differences. And that's true of the Japanese-collectivism, American-individualism stereotype, as well.

In reality, many (if not most) Americans are not as individualistic as they, or the Japanese, think. America has its anarchistic loners, to be sure. But tens of millions of Americans live their lives cocooned in supportive networks of groups: families, churches, companies, communities.

Nor are all Japanese sheeplike conformists with suppressed personalities, unable to function on their own. The foreigner who spends even a few months in Japan learns that the individual variations are as important as the shared traits.

The truth is that true individuals who march only to their own drum are rare in any society—but Japan has its share. Whether any of the Japanese profiled in this section qualify as true individuals is probably a moot point. But all of them qualify as unusual people, not to mention unusual Japanese. In that sense, they are a powerful rebuttal to the stereotypical denial of Japanese individualism.

* * *

'Pink Lady' May Just Be Japan's Leading Eccentric

EDITOR'S NOTE: "England is the paradise of individuality, eccentricity, heresy, anomalies, hobbies and humours," said George Santayana, the famous philosopher. Did he say England? For sheer individuality, eccentricity and anomalies, few Englishwomen measure up to Masako Ohya, the subject of our next story.

MUROU—When the "pink lady" plays golf, she doesn't mind showing a little thigh.

Every time Masako Ohya swings her pink club, her frilly miniskirt swirls around her ample waist, exposing her bloomers and her opaque pink tights.

Scandalous? Not for the 70-year-old Madame Ohya, as some of her foreign friends call her. That is how the Japanese heiress always dresses on the green, whether at St. Andrew's in Scotland or in a friendship match with pro golfer Severiano Ballesteros.

"I got the hint from a ballet costume," explains Mrs. Ohya in one of her six autobiographies. "I've been learning ballet since I was little, so I think nothing of showing my legs."

Japan has a growing number of eccentric rich people, but for sheer extravagance and idiosyncrasy few can match Mrs.

Ohya—businesswoman, fanatical golfer, singer, ballet-school owner, self-promoter, lover of attention and the color pink.

She owns more than 4,000 dresses—90% of them pink.

The squeaky-voiced Mrs. Ohya has long been a well-known—and somewhat buffoonish—figure on Japanese TV talk shows. A few years back, she would go on television with her cheeks painted pink, dance with aerobics instructors, say indiscreet things about sex and make a spectacle of herself generally. Now she has gone international. She's an honorary citizen of Trenton, New Jersey, and has 21 awards from various nations, including the Legion of Honor from France.

That appalls some Japanese, who consider her an embarrassment to the nation. Moriyuki Motono, Japan's former ambassador to France, says he excused himself from the opening ceremony of an arts festival in Paris when he learned Mrs. Ohya was also attending. "I told the French minister," he says, "that though it may be impolite, there is someone here whom I don't wish to be identified with at an official event."

Mr. Motono says he also has refused to take time to meet her during her frequent appearances in Paris. He says Mrs. Ohya once had the effrontery to take a TV crew to a formal dinner given by Princess Caroline of Monaco.

Mrs. Ohya doesn't like the ambassador either and denounced him in her memoirs. But for the most part, she is unfazed by criticism, particularly the suggestion that she is ostentatious.

She owns more than 4,000 dresses—90% of them pink. She stopped counting her hats when she got to 500, she giggles. Her arresting wardrobe includes rosy haute couture by Ungaro, Dior and Balmain, in addition to some pink things of her own design. She always wears a hat of some pink shade (or a magenta veil) and 10-centimeter platform shoes to bring her height closer to 150 centimeters.

Last year, she toured Paris arm-in-arm with Danielle Mitterrand, the wife of the French president, in a baggy fuchsia gown and a wreath of pink fake flowers. (Mrs. Ohya had paid $100,000 for a dinner party after a charity bash sponsored by Mrs. Mitterrand's foundation.)

"There's no one who can meet people wearing clothes as original as Ms. Ohya," says Jyunsuke Shimada, who began working in Ms. Ohya's cherry-pink business office 10 years ago after retiring as a professional baseball player.

Mrs. Ohya makes the most of every meeting with a celebrity, even chance encounters in hotel lobbies. Her personal photographer, ever at her side, snaps pictures of every conceivably noteworthy moment. Thus, there is recorded proof that she has been kissed by Adnan Khashoggi. Of course, there are lots of golf shots since the game is her great passion. (Her score for nine holes averages 48, she boasts.)

At the end of each year, Mrs. Ohya puts her favorite snapshots in a 400-page picture book she gives out to people who visit the golf club she owns in Murou, about 350 kilometers southeast of Tokyo.

Doing It for Daddy

Why all the pink? In her rose-colored batik robe one night, Mrs. Ohya explains that, though she actually prefers white and blue, she wears pink to please her late husband, Shinzo, who died in 1980 at the age of 86.

"Daddy," as she calls him, loved pink. And she has heard from his ghost. She made the mistake of wearing blue once after her husband's death. "Daddy got mad. So I went back to wearing rose," she grins.

Her obsession with pink definitely extends to the Murou Royal Country Club, Mrs. Ohya's principal business in Japan. Fuchsia billboards bloom in the quiet rice paddies of this rural town near Osaka, to direct visitors to the club, whose 2,500 members stride through a rose-carpeted hallway to relax on magenta sofas. Players record their golf scores on salmon-pink score cards and eat on wine-colored tablecloths. A clubhouse museum has walls of pink.

Mrs. Ohya has used the fortune she inherited from her late husband to build a substantial business but won't comment on the scale of it all. She does say her two golf courses in Japan are worth more than $300 million and that she recently bought a course in Britain for $16 million.

Her businesses include two real-estate agencies, a hospital, gasoline stations and a fleet of taxis. She is the director of two Japanese restaurant chains in Europe (K.K. Yakitori and Cardinal Entertainment Business Ltd.). Her ballet school has 300 students (10 of whom she recently took to perform in Bulgaria).

But it's golf that keeps her in the pink. Two years ago, Mrs. Ohya bought a 17th-century chateau in the suburbs of Paris and turned it into a hotel (the Chateau d'Humiere Masako-Ohya) with golf links in the back yards.

The daughter of a wealthy politician, she sang professionally in a chorus before marrying Shinzo Ohya in 1949. He was a budding politician 26 years her senior. He ultimately became Japan's construction minister and finance minister, as well as president of Teijin Ltd., the nation's largest maker of polyester.

Her husband encouraged her real-estate investments, and because certain golf courses refused to admit women, he encouraged her to build her own, which she did.

Being a woman, especially a woman done up in pink, made it difficult to do business with men, says Mrs. Ohya. "Forty years ago, I was bullied by a hundred people," she says. "I was smiling during the day, but I always cried at night."

But she built her business. She frequented bars and sold golf-course memberships to tipsy executives who mistook her for a bar hostess. Some say she traded on her husband's power. When Mr. Ohya was president of the polyester company, "There were few who stuck their noses into everything like Masako Ohya," says Makoto Sataka, a Tokyo management critic.

Mineral Baths

Mrs. Ohya, who is still a major shareholder of Teijin, which had sales of $2.36 billion in 1989, contends that the money she made was entirely her own doing. "I pay 10 times as much tax as Daddy used to," she says. But the chirpy tycoon immediately goes silent when asked for details. That doesn't mean she isn't actively engaged in her businesses or that she can't keep businessmen cooling their heels outside her door waiting for her to finish with still other businessmen.

At least, for now, the energetic Mrs. Ohya has no plans to retire. She keeps her skin supple, it is said, by taking mineral baths. She is fit enough to play 36 holes of golf and beats the businessmen she plays with.

What keeps Mrs. Ohya zipping around the world is overflowing self-confidence, complete indifference to criticism and, finally, utter insouciance about how she speaks English. She has a pet phrase to remind herself to keep going. And she chants it proudly: "From now start, never too late."

— YUMIKO ONO

January 4, 1991

* * *

Japan's Egg King Scrambles to the Top of U.S. Market

EDITOR'S NOTE: In this profile of Japan's "Egg King," an American expert on Japanese literature says the king is drawn to the U.S. because "there are a lot more people like him in America than in Japan." Maybe. No doubt Americans in general are more individualistic than Japanese. But there aren't very many people anywhere with the Ayn Randish independence of some of Japan's strongest individuals. The Egg King is very much a case in point.

TOYAMA—The average Japanese eats fewer eggs than people in some other countries.

The average Westerner isn't surprised about that when he contemplates how the average Japanese eat their eggs—raw, over rice with seaweed or as a dip for sukiyaki, or in a cold omelet ribboned with seaweed in a sushi bar.

But egg consumption has been rising in Japan, at least partly thanks to the energetic efforts of Hikonobu Ise, who has come to be known as Japan's egg king. Running the family egg business founded by his father here near the Japan Sea, the 53-year-old Mr. Ise rapidly expanded all over the country, to attain a dominant 4% of the Japanese egg market.

Like many of his fellow businessmen from this part of the world, Mr. Ise soon began scrambling for new business in the West. But unlike some of them, he doesn't pay his workers chicken feed, and he didn't devise a technologically superior or more productive hen. There may be a robot gap, but there isn't any egg gap.

Friendly Invasion

What Mr. Ise did was to team up with a Mississippi egg expert and a Japanese-speaking Wall Street lawyer to hatch a U.S. egg business. In 1980, he acquired Seaboard Foods Inc. in New Jersey. Since then, he has bought egg businesses in Virginia, Florida, South Carolina, Pennsylvania and Indiana. The eggs he sells are 100% local content and will continue to be, he says, although he isn't sure how much further he will expand his U.S. egg empire. He says his lawyer, Isaac Shapiro, a partner at Milbank Tweed Hadley & McCloy and a former president of the Japan Society in New York, would like to see him diversify.

> *"If you've never been chewed out by a fellow who can't speak much English and is a foot shorter than you—well, he's good at it," an American egg man says.*

"Every time I propose a takeover," Mr. Ise says, "Mr. Shapiro replies, 'I don't want to deal with the chickens anymore. Why don't you buy some nice real estate in Manhattan?'" Mr. Ise adds with mock gravity, "He's a bad lawyer."

Mr. Shapiro replies, "I have nothing against chickens or eggs whatsoever. It may be that in the past I said to him, 'Don't you, like, think you should diversify? Don't you think—excuse me—that maybe you shouldn't put all of your eggs in one basket?' I may have said that, but Manhattan real estate was his idea."

It took a shrewd businessman like Mr. Ise, with exceptional self-assurance and a keen sense of humor, to make eggs more popular in Japan. The very concept of trading in eggs was unknown in Japan until a century ago. The ancient Japanese raised chickens only to show them off in competitions. As recently as a generation ago, some Japanese regarded an egg as something to take to a sick friend instead of flowers.

To help hasten the egg revolution in Japan, Mr. Ise personally eats three to five eggs a day and never misses a chance to say something nice about an egg. He is horrified, for example, by the fear some Americans have about the cholesterol in eggs, a fear he blames on "Eisenhower's doctor," who drew attention to the issue by limiting the late president's egg intake for health reasons.

Mr. Ise's interest in eggs started on the family farm. In 1931, about the time he was born, an Ise chicken set a world record by laying 338 eggs in a year, according to family lore (although the Guinness Book of World Records says a New Zealand hen ruled the roost, having laid 361 eggs in 1930).

With five million Ise chickens now supplying eggs in Japan, a Japanese book recently described Mr. Ise as *Nihon no eggu o,* Japan's egg king. (The Japanese word for egg is *tamago,* but Japanese sometimes inexplicably use Japanized English words like eggu.)

In rising to that exalted position, Mr. Ise hasn't necessarily won the acclaim of his competitors. Tadaichi Serita, another leading egg producer in Japan, calls Mr. Ise "selfish" and "lacking common sense" for having refused to go along with a government-supported price-setting scheme. He was summoned to the parliament in 1979 to explain his position, and as he was testifying that he didn't see anything wrong with selling eggs at low prices, 1,000 farmers demonstrated against him in front of the parliament building.

Never in the U.S.
"That kind of thing would never happen in the U.S.," Mr. Ise says.

Not only does Mr. Ise find the relative openness of the American market to his liking, he finds the openness of Americans to his liking as well. Among the many objects of art in his sprawling house is an Andy Warhol group portrait of the directors of his American operations—a portrait that reportedly cost $50,000. Mr. Ise devotes 10% of his U.S. profits to a foundation he set up to improve U.S.-Japan understanding. Its first project is to try to improve the treatment of each country in the other's school textbooks.

"I think he responds to America because he finds there are a lot more people like himself in America than in Japan," says Donald Keene, an expert on Japanese literature who is a member of the foundation's board. Mr. Keene adds that Mr. Ise's "most unusual quality as a Japanese is that he seems to be absolutely without inhibitions."

"He's attracted to things that are foreign in a good sense," says Mr. Shapiro, his lawyer. "He has a kind of wonderment about the world. He isn't at all allergic to foreigners, because he's confident in himself."

Several years ago, Mr. Ise met Mr. Shapiro, who grew up in Japan, where his parents taught music. He later asked Mr. Shapiro to help find U.S. egg businesses to acquire. Mr. Ise also asked Mr. Shapiro to look after the family of his son-in-law, whom he had dispatched to the U.S. and who is now a vice president of Seaboard Foods. "I don't know how good a lawyer he [Shapiro] is, but he's great at taking care of grandchildren," Mr. Ise says. Mr. Shapiro replies, "We do have an unusual relationship for a lawyer and client—it's sort of a family friendship."

Through Mr. Shapiro, Mr. Ise eventually met Fred Adams, a Jackson, Mississippi, egg man. Mr. Ise wanted to buy Mr. Adams's business, one of America's largest, but Mr. Adams convinced him there were better opportunities up North. The egg business was moving back North in response to rising freight rates. For years, some egg distributors had supplied the Midwest and Eastern markets from the South because it was cheaper to do it that way.

Today, Mr. Adams spends half his time running his own business and half helping run Seaboard for Mr. Ise. The two egg men get along fine. "If you've never been chewed out by a fellow who can't speak much English and is a foot shorter than you—well, he's good at it," Mr. Adams says with a chuckle.

The secret of Mr. Ise's success in the U.S. has been aggressiveness rather than technique, Mr. Adams explains. "There isn't very much difference between the egg business in Japan and the egg business in the U.S.," he says. "They use the same breeding stock, the same equipment, the same feed formulation." If anything, the U.S. has a cost advantage because Japan has to import so much of its chicken feed from America. Mr. Ise says he would export eggs from the U.S. back to Japan if it weren't for the informal trade barriers in Japan.

Actually, there are some differences between the two countries. Roosters in the U.S. say cock-a-doodle-do, but Japanese roosters say *ko-ke-ko-kko*. Japanese chickens' chicken feed contains a little fish meal. Also, unlike in the U.S., in Japan there isn't any argument about which came first, the chicken or the egg. It was unquestionably the chicken, Mr. Ise asserts. His rationale: In old Japanese art, you see lots of pictures of women wearing kimonos decorated with chickens (the ancient Japanese thought chickens were beautiful) but none decorated with eggs.

Whatever the differences, though, there is a common denominator in the two countries' egg markets: Mr. Ise. He claims 25% of the Tokyo egg market, 15% of New York's. His 4% of the Japanese egg market overall now matches his share of the U.S. egg market overall. As Mr. Adams says, "In two short years Ise and his affiliates have emerged as No. 1 in the U.S. egg market." In other words, you may now call Mr. Ise "America no eggu o."

— URBAN C. LEHNER

June 30, 1983

* * *

Veteran Japanese Golfer Goes For the Course Record

EDITOR'S NOTE: If single-mindedness is characteristic of individualists, you can add Tatsuo Yamashita's name to the list. Mr. Yamashita is a man with a mission, and his obsessiveness in pursuit of his goal is a thing to behold. "For Mr. Yamashita," the next story explains, "a golf course is not a place to test ability or show off wealth. It's a thing to be checked off a list."

ASHIKAGA CITY—Tatsuo Yamashita strides onto the green, lines up his putt and knocks it home, breaking his own national record.

His score for the day? Don't ask. When it's over 100, Mr. Yamashita doesn't keep track. The record this 71-year-old retired naval engineer is going for has nothing to do with how well he plays.

With a bearing reminiscent of the medieval warriors who once swaggered through these parts, Mr. Yamashita thrusts out his chest, plants a club at his side and bellows to his startled caddy: "That's 1,731 courses. I'm out to conquer every one in the country."

Even in this nation of golf fanatics, Mr. Yamashita has a singular drive. And he attends to it in his own modest way. He doesn't go in for fancy golf duds, preferring a gray, long-sleeved golf shirt and a pair of plain dark slacks. Bad shots never make him angry. At most, his jaw gets a little tighter if he hooks into the woods or lands in a sand trap. He uses only six clubs, which he keeps in a slim, synthetic bag. He favors his four-wood.

> *"Some people want to ride all the railroads in Japan. Others want to visit all the shrines. Me, I want to play all the golf courses."*

For Mr. Yamashita, a golf course is not a place to test ability or show off wealth. It is a thing to be checked off a list. "Some people want to ride all the railroads in Japan. Others want to visit all the shrines. Me, I want to play all the golf courses," he says. "It gives me a goal in life. Not many people my age have one."

Mr. Yamashita took up the game in 1962. Like many enthusiastic beginners, he entertained visions of becoming a scratch golfer. But when he couldn't get his handicap lower than 17, he altered his sights. "If I couldn't be the best, I figured I could play the most," he says.

In 1985 alone, Mr. Yamashita hooked and sliced his way through 173 courses. You can look it up in the ledger where he inscribes in neat rows the name of every course he plays. His log charts his march through the countryside, and also the boom-and-bust cycles of Japanese golf.

To Mr. Yamashita, these cycles present opportunities. Between 1960 and the early '70s, 750 courses sprang up, which gave him plenty to conquer. Then the 1973 oil crisis ushered in hard times. This was more good news. With country clubs struggling to stay afloat, "members were gods, visitors were Buddhas, and anyone with a discount guest ticket got a royal welcome," Mr. Yamashita recalls. "That period lasted until about 1985, and that's when I built up my total."

Then came the late 1980s, when the price of golf memberships spiraled to dizzying heights as speculators raced to build the most lavish, most elite courses. "Nowadays, if you're not a moneybags, some places don't want to have anything to do with you," Mr. Yamashita huffs.

But he also says the new snobbery may have put his dream out of reach for any would-be challengers, though none has surfaced. And his track record still opens most doors. Only in the "one in 100" case where a stuffy club has refused to let him play as a special guest, is he forced to spend as much as a year searching out a member to sponsor him.

On a recent fine day, Mr. Yamashita has set his sights on Tsutsujigaoka (Azalea Hills) Country Club, about a two hours' drive north of Tokyo. Like many of the newest courses in this land-scarce nation, this one was literally blasted out of a ridge. Soil was scraped from the site's marshy lowlands and spread over the rocky terraces that now serve as fairways.

Everything is steep at this club. A lifetime membership costs $350,000. And the paths between greens and tees are so formidable that half are equipped with so-called autoslopes, push-button conveyor belts that carry golfers up or down to the next hole. To get to the 18th tee, Mr. Yamashita and his two pals must mount an autoslope, then pile into a funicular gondola for the final 90 meters.

The course is tended as meticulously as a bonsai tree. The young woman who serves as caddy scurries to repair divots with sand troweled from a canvas bucket that hangs on her automated pushcart. Halfway through the front nine, Mr.

Yamashita and his buddies step inside a shady, wooden pavilion to cool off with chilled hand towels and free drinks.

To a onetime caddy in one of New York's tonier suburbs, the sprawling Tsutsujigaoka clubhouse is stunning. Its two-story lobby is paneled in Italian marble. Its airy dressing room opens into a stone-floored chamber with 14 meters of marble-bordered Japanese baths. They look out onto a miniature pond framed by a distant mountain ridge.

But Mr. Yamashita, a bluff man with a quick mind and a curmudgeonly style, isn't impressed. A "third-class" facility, he harrumphs: The fairways are too narrow, the distance between holes is too long and the clubhouse is far less lavish than many. He rates the twin waterfall that cascades over boulders into a pond alongside the practice green as "not the best, but among the top two or three [golf-course] waterfalls."

Because he has so much ground to cover every year, Mr. Yamashita plans his itinerary carefully. Toward the end of the year, he buys a new-course guidebook, put out by K.K. Golf Digest, a leading publisher of Japanese golf magazines. Then he bolts for northern Japan before the first snow and works his way south, trying to hit all the new courses before more open when the weather warms. "Then, for a brief time, I can say I've played them all." He fell a few courses behind last year, and must play about 90 courses before mid-1992 to catch up.

For the most part, Mr. Yamashita has figured out how to play on the cheap. He travels by train and taxi and stays in inexpensive hotels. Including lunch and caddy fee, it typically costs him 25,000 yen or so for a weekday visit at clubs in greater Tokyo. In more rural regions, the average is closer to 15,000 yen. Mr. Yamashita often plays for half price or less, as many clubs allow him to play at members' rates. (Yes, even members pay greens fees.) Since he isn't a household name yet, he often writes the club a letter explaining his goal in life and this can result in a red-carpet treatment of sorts. At Tsutsujigaoka, the managing director offered him green tea, a chat and a bow.

At home in Tokyo, Mr. Yamashita hangs out in a neighborhood coffee shop with electronic games built into the tables and golf balls embedded in the ashtrays. He lives in a dim condominium of four cramped rooms. In one, he displays caps, belts, tie pins, ashtrays and other golf mementos.

But he can't afford to spend too much time there. With 378 more golf courses under construction and an additional 1,073 on the drawing boards, according to the Japan Golf Association, Mr. Yamashita's target will keep moving for the rest of the century, though many of the planned courses will probably be scrapped. That's fine with Mr. Yamashita, who admits that the recent pace of 80 or so new courses a year has been a bit hectic.

Besides, "golf isn't fun for me anymore," he barks. "The only fun is extending my record."

— CHRISTOPHER J. CHIPELLO

November 4, 1991

* * *

TV Rabble-Rouser Helped Topple 'The Don' of Japanese Politics

EDITOR'S NOTE: In Japan, unlike in many other countries, the anchorman on the evening news is often a plain-vanilla, button-down, eminently forgettable character, a mere reader of news. Not Hiroshi Kume. He's a showman, a crusader, a pundit, a popularizer and, most importantly, a personality. And not only is he revolutionizing television news in Japan; he's showing, once again, that there's nothing inherently un-Japanese about being one's own person.

TOKYO—"I might be killed," Japan's most-popular news anchor, Hiroshi Kume, told millions of startled viewers recently at the end of his report on Japan's political scandal. "Gangsters are involved."

Mr. Kume may lay it on a bit thick, but that's a big part of his tremendous public appeal here.

Mr. Kume may have been laying it on a bit thick, but that's a big part of his tremendous public appeal here. It also explains how he has helped transform Japanese news reporting—and perhaps Japanese democracy—in the process.

Mr. Kume is as given to flamboyant antics as serious journalism. Once, he held up photos of Ronald Reagan and Noboru Takeshita to show how short the Japanese prime minister looked next to the U.S. president. Another time, he shaved his head when his favorite baseball team lost the Japanese pennant. And when the news displeases him, Mr. Kume sometimes stares into the camera and asks his viewers, "What on earth is happening to Japan?"

So last Wednesday, when one of Japan's top politicians resigned in disgrace from the Diet, people here wondered whether Mr. Kume was as responsible as anyone for helping bring him down.

Corruption has long gone hand-in-hand with Japanese politics, so few in this nation were shocked in late August when 78-year-old Shin Kanemaru, dubbed "the don" and considered Japan's most powerful political boss, admitted to taking $4 million in illegal campaign contributions from a mob-affiliated trucking company. The prosecutors let him off with a slap on the wrist—a $1,700 fine.

It was Japan's oft-ignored, oft-docile public opinion, whipped up by the likes of Mr. Kume, that prodded Mr. Kanemaru from office. Mr. Kanemaru's twists and turns have been displayed on Mr. Kume's top-rated nightly show, peppered by Mr. Kume's sarcastic cracks and gestures.

"Everyone, do you think that's acceptable?" Mr. Kume has said in the past, leaning into the camera.

It turns out that most Japanese don't.

When the Kanemaru scandal broke, it seemed likely to unfold the way so many had before: A top politician gives up a title, but retains tremendous power behind the scenes. After a month of seclusion, Mr. Kanemaru re-emerged, mumbled to the press that he would never do it again and, with that, headed off to the office.

But not for long. Mr. Kume began featuring the Kanemaru scandal nightly. Describing Mr. Kanemaru's admission, Mr. Kume once gestured as if stuffing his pockets with cash. Then, using a map of Japan, Mr. Kume showed viewers those areas where local assemblies had condemned Mr. Kanemaru. When Mr. Kanemaru's home district stuck by their man, rejecting a resolution calling for greater political ethics, Mr. Kume conducted a poll of the area and triumphantly reported that 80% of respondents said Mr. Kanemaru should quit.

In the weeks since Mr. Kanemaru's crime came to light, demonstrators have, among other things, thrown paint at the prosecutors' office and collected thousands of protest signatures. A magazine last week published an article by an army major urging a military coup to "purify" the government.

Polls showed that nearly 90% of Japanese thought Mr.

Kanemaru should give up his post. Many factors helped stir the outrage, but Mr. Kume and his antics may have been near the top of the list. "The opposition parties were supposed to demand Kanemaru's explanation [for his actions], but they didn't do it," says Kengo Kanazawa, who publishes a weekly media newsletter. "So the news media did." Mr. Kume's show, he says, is "overwhelming."

"I like Mr. Kume's clear way of saying things," Fusako Iwase, a 69-year-old retired schoolteacher said Wednesday, while collecting signatures for an anti-Kanemaru petition. "I feel like applauding" during his commentary.

Mr. Kume is an unlikely cheerleader for Japan's reluctant masses. The 48-year-old Tokyo-area native became a national figure as co-host of "The Best 10," a pop-music review in which he played the straightman to a fast-talking female co-host. Before he burst on the scene with his news show seven years ago, his sort of news was unheard of. The stodgy, quasi-governmental network NHK set the tone.

Then in 1985, TV Asahi, struggling in the ratings, gave Mr. Kume a chance. The anchor didn't hesitate to break from journalistic ranks. His favorite American newscaster, he once told an interviewer, is late-night talk-show host David Letterman; today, his show opens with a montage of a whale, a frying pan and other objects floating through skyscrapers.

Mr. Kume wouldn't grant an interview for this article. But one of his producers says Mr. Kume sets out "to deliver news in a very easy form, to make it understandable even for junior-high-school students." Indeed, Mr. Kume is praised for distilling complex issues to their essentials; in a nation where few people, political or otherwise, make direct appeals to the public, he may be Japan's greatest communicator.

He's also a master showman. During the failed Soviet coup, he brought a grinning wax model of Mikhail Gorbachev into the studio to show viewers the man involved. Height seems to be of concern to Mr. Kume. After playing a clip from the first U.S. presidential debate early last week, Mr. Kume observed that Ross Perot would be the most compatible, at least in size, with current Prime Minister Kiichi Miyazawa.

The public eats it up. Mr. Kume's show is the country's top-rated news program and has spawned a number of imitators. "There's no doubt he has influenced the format," says Seiichi Kanise, who anchors a Sunday news show on rival Tokyo Broadcasting System Inc. "He's established his own style of talking directly to the public, not as a journalist."

Some Japanese think Mr. Kume has gone too far. Earlier this year, a cabinet minister urged people to boycott advertisers on Mr. Kume's show for its coverage of legislation to send Japanese peacekeeping troops abroad. Mr. Kume's simplicity "is very dangerous," says Naoyuki Arai, a journalism professor at Souka University. "Young people are convinced because Mr. Kume says so. I think that's a problem."

With Mr. Kanemaru gone, Japan now wonders whether the scandal will die, or whether the nation's timid "people power" will touch other politicians. If Mr. Kume has anything to say about it, it will. He devoted much of last Wednesday night's broadcast to the widely suspected involvement in the scandal of former Prime Minister Takeshita, and trumpeted his station's instant poll results that showed 70% of respondents believed Mr. Takeshita should also quit the Diet.

"Unless public opinion and the mass media push hard, there won't be the desired political reforms," a commentator said to Mr. Kume during that broadcast. "Henceforth, public opinion and journalism will become more important." Mr. Kume then clenched his fists, solemnly bowed to the camera and said, "Indeed, thank you very much."

— JACOB M. SCHLESINGER and MASAYOSHI KANABAYASHI
October 19, 1992

SECTION SIX

A NATION OF
INTERNATIONALISTS

Introduction

It doesn't happen often in Tokyo anymore, but a foreigner visiting a country town may still find himself pursued by schoolchildren yelling *haro,* hello, and *gaijin,* foreigner.

"I often see Japanese parents teaching their children to point and say 'gaijin' in the same way that they teach them to point and say 'panda' or 'monkey' at the zoo," complains a foreign resident of Japan in the opening story of this section.

The Japanese have long been famed for their insularity. Millennia of living on a racially homogeneous island have instilled a deeply ingrained sense that the world is divided into two kinds—Japanese and all others. And while the trait is not as extreme with the Japanese as it is with some American Indian tribes, who reserve the word "human being" for their fellow tribesmen, it can still drive gaijin to distraction.

Even gaijin who know the country well, like Edward Seidensticker, one of the premier translators of Japanese literature. The Japanese "are not like other people," he wrote in a column in Tokyo's Yomiuri newspaper in 1958. "They are infinitely more clannish, insular, parochial, and one owes it to one's self-respect to preserve a feeling of outrage at the insularity." Fearing that he was losing his sense of outrage, Mr. Seidensticker announced in that column that he was leaving Japan after many years of residing in the country.

And yet, as Mr. Seidensticker knew and as the stories in this section make clear, Japanese attitudes toward the world outside the Japanese archipelago are too complex to be reduced to the single word "insularity."

This is a society that has adopted Buddhism, Confucianism and a system of writing from China. It is a society where Western jazz artists often draw bigger crowds than they do in the West. A society that likes Caucasian models in its advertising, that spends (mostly to little avail) enormous sums every year on English lessons and that fills its bookstores with idealistic tomes on the need for *kokusaika,* internationalization.

Indeed, students of other East Asian societies have long marveled at Japan's willingness in the 19th century to adopt liberally from the West when confronted with the threat of Western colonialism. The Chinese, faced with the same threat, tried to adopt Western technology without adopting Western ideas and institutions, writes Gordon Redding in "The Spirit of Chinese Capitalism." They failed.

Meanwhile, Japan went on what Dr. Redding calls "an open-minded searching for new models of law, education, military structures, etc., all of which were carefully absorbed into a state which succeeded in remaining true to itself."

Today, too, the Japanese manage to make everything they do seem distinctly Japanese even while they continue to adopt liberally from other countries. They continue to be curious about the outside world, but also baffled and occasionally repelled by its refusal to conform to Japanese norms. And for every book on internationalization, they seem to produce another celebrating their own cultural and even racial uniqueness.

* * *

Is Japan Polite or Rude? It Depends Who You Ask

EDITOR'S NOTE: In the summer of 1994, a Japanese television network ran a special program featuring foreigners singing karaoke in Japanese. Can anyone imagine an American or European network thinking there would be an audience for a program consisting of Japanese singing in English? Yet foreigners have long been objects of curiosity in Japan, which sometimes means they're treated well indeed. Other times, they bridle at being treated "like a dog with two legs instead of four," as the next story recounts.

TOKYO—W.G. Scheerer, who recently visited Japan for the second time in nine years, considers the Japanese the world's friendliest, most polite people. "Complete strangers from many walks of life and of many ages have been not only courteous but helpful and friendly to me," says the Holmdel, New Jersey, resident.

> *"If a foreigner speaks Japanese he's a curiosity: a two-legged dog who also happens to speak Japanese."*

Cathleen Parks, who has been teaching English for two years in the remote city of Kitakyushu, doesn't consider the Japanese polite at all. "Japanese people seem to think that foreigners are animals with no human feelings," she complains. Bernard Ross, who lives north of Tokyo in Mito, says he is "tired of being treated like a zoo animal" and plans to move to "a less falsely polite country."

Debates Rage
That is one of the paradoxes of this paradoxical nation. The Japanese are renowned world-wide for their hospitality to foreign visitors. Yet some foreigners who live here think, as the Japan expert Jack Seward once wrote, that "the Japanese may well be the rudest people on God's green globe."

Not all foreign residents feel that way. Opinion polls suggest that a majority find Japan and the Japanese congenial. Debates on the issue frequently rage in the letters column of the Japan Times, the largest (circulation 50,000) of the four English-language dailies published here. (W.G. Scheerer, Cathleen Parks and Bernard Ross voiced the opinions quoted earlier in one such debate a couple of months ago; another has begun since then.)

Garrett Flint, a Brunswick Corp. vice president who has lived in Japan 25 years, says the at-best ambivalent attitudes toward foreigners here are "one of the recurring topics of conversation" among foreign residents. With more and more foreigners living in Japan these days—about 125,600, up 30% from a decade ago—that ambivalence could take on increasing importance in shaping international attitudes.

It is easy to see how the Japanese got their reputation for warmth and courtesy. Hotel and restaurant workers and office receptionists meet the visiting foreigner with bows and smiles. (At one Tokyo hotel, a coy young woman helpfully coos "this is robby" to foreigners as they get off the elevator at the lobby floor.) If the foreigner tries to stumble through a few words of Japanese from a phrasebook, people gush at his command of the language.

Guests and Outsiders

What the tourist doesn't realize, the critics of Japanese manners say, is that tourists are *okyakusan,* guests, and thus entitled to the best of treatment. Foreigners who live in Japan, on the other hand, are no longer for most purposes okyakusan. They are simply outsiders.

As such, they will at times feel like freaks. "I often see Japanese parents teaching their children to point and say *'gaijin,'* foreigner, in the same way that they teach them to point and say 'panda' or 'monkey' at the zoo," Miss Parks complains. She says she can't "enjoy a simple stroll . . . without being followed by schoolboys shouting 'haro, haro,' hello, and 'I know my ABCs.'"

At other times they will feel rejected. "Many foreigners have difficulty getting integrated in Japan," says Tadashi Yamamoto, the head of the Japan Center for International Exchange, a private group that tries to promote person-to-person contacts between Japanese and foreigners. "I often hear foreigners say things like, 'After five years here I don't have a single Japanese I can really call a buddy.'" Mastering the difficulties of the Japanese language doesn't necessarily help. "To the Japanese, a foreigner is a curiosity, a dog with two legs instead of four," says an American graduate student here writing a doctoral thesis on Japanese education. "If the foreigner speaks Japanese, he is even more of a curiosity: a two-legged dog who also happens to speak Japanese."

The complaint—and the use of animal metaphors—is an old one. "Seeing that you speak Japanese," the British Japanologist Basil Hall Chamberlain wrote in 1904, "they will wag their heads and smile condescendingly, and admit to each other that you are really quite intelligent—much as we might do in the presence of the learned pig or an ape of somewhat unusual attainments."

Some of these problems, even the critics concede, crop up in adjusting to any foreign culture. The complaining foreigners' letters to the Japan Times invariably draw responses from other foreigners suggesting that anyone who doesn't like Japan is free to leave it. Many Japanese, for their part, are surprised at the foreigners' thin skin.

"I would be happy to be looked at as if I were a panda in a zoo," says Kiyoaki Murata, the Japan Times's editor. "In Japan, the panda is an honored animal." The Japanese, Mr. Murata says, are "generally polite," but they take "natural human interest in anything novel."

However, the foreign complainers retort that Japan, with its we-they mentality, is unusually hard on outsiders. Even the term gaijin, literally just a neutral word for foreigner, gets used in a way that offends many. "My children are always asking me what gaijin means," says a South Asian businessman here. "I tell them it just means foreigner, but they say, 'Daddy, what does it really mean?'"

One American reporter posted to Tokyo a few years ago didn't realize how it affected his children until he took them on vacation to Hawaii. There they retaliated by running up and down the beach yelling gaijin at Japanese children.

Taxi Dancing
Seemingly little things annoy foreigners here. An American man tells of standing in line for train tickets and having Japanese barge in front of him "as if I weren't there." (Japanese make the same complaint.) The American man also recalls that on his first day in his Tokyo neighborhood, he put his garbage out for collection in a plastic bag, unaware that paper bags were required. Within minutes came a knock on the door, and soon he found himself in the street at the garbage-collection point, surrounded by neighbors and being treated to a long lecture on garbage protocol. "It felt like a lynch mob," he says.

Another American, infuriated for years by the mysterious refusal of Tokyo cab drivers to pick up foreigners during certain late-night hours, confesses that he once lost his temper and kicked in the side of a taxi.

Celia Farnon touched off the latest debate in the Japan Times with yet another complaint: Japanese practicing English. She says she has "been rudely interrupted on a number of occasions" by Japanese who seem to think that "foreigners are walking language teachers/dictionaries that may be approached for a free lesson at any time."

Sexual harassment is also a common complaint of foreign women. Though less likely to become victims of rape here than in the U.S. or Europe, they tell of frequent pinching and feeling on crowded trains. According to one, perhaps apocryphal, story, a Western woman turned the tables on one subway fondler by grabbing his hand, holding it aloft and loudly demanding, "Whose hand is this?"

Western women also seem to bring out the exhibitionist and flasher tendencies in Japanese men. And many complain of crude propositions by passers-by. "I have been asked many times how much I 'charge' to the point that I border on the permanent defensive," says Deborah Smith, an Associated Press reporter here.

Help From a Jogger

But for every such tale of woe, there seems to be a counterstory of Japanese kindness and courtesy. Almost every foreigner here has had the experience of having something lost returned to him. An American jogger in Tokyo didn't notice recently that his wallet had slipped out of his pocket. But a Japanese man did and picked it up. He jogged after the American to return it.

Ron Linden, a visiting British professor in a small town north of Tokyo, tells of another common occurrence, the Japanese eagerness to help direct the foreigner who looks even vaguely lost. On one train trip with his wife, "to prevent our worrying, a passenger drew a diagram for us showing exactly where our station was on the line," he says. "On our way on foot through a village on the slopes of Mount Tsukuba, we lost our way at one point. The correct route was pointed out by two very young children. All of this assistance, by young and old, was unsolicited by us; everyone simply assumed that we might be in difficulties."

When Jackson Huddleston, an American businessman of

long experience in Japan, was returning from a camping trip in northern Japan recently, he had difficulty making train and plane connections and found himself stranded in isolated cities for several hours. A Japanese man and an unrelated Japanese woman having similar difficulties proceeded to "adopt" him, even though he was still dressed in his shabby camping garb and even though he made it clear he could speak and read Japanese and thus fend for himself. "For several hours, we were like a family," Mr. Huddleston recalls fondly.

— URBAN C. LEHNER

August 4, 1982

* * *

Japan Gives Free Rein to Foreign Architects

EDITOR'S NOTE: In Europe or America, notes a foreign architect in the following story, "It will be difficult to build an enormous concrete rock building like Noah's Ark." In Japan, especially during the "bubble" years of the late 1980s and early 1990s, any bizarre creation could be built, as long as a foreign architect designed it. Needless to say, foreign architects loved this. They flocked to Japan, not only for the fat commissions, but for the chance to design structures that would never get past the zoning board back home.

TOKYO—Amid a huddle of grubby bars and noodle stalls in northern Tokyo rises a monstrous, glittering, pear-shaped blob tipped on its side.

"I didn't know what to make of it at first," concedes Yoshinobu Takeda, a spokesman for Asahi Breweries Ltd., owner of the 44-meter-long structure perched atop a boxlike black building. Speculation among local residents about the nature of the golden dollop ranged from a giant drop of beer to more earthy objects.

> *The blob—or flame, rather—is one of about 60 wacky structures recently built or now going up in Japan that were designed by foreign architects.*

Actually, the structure—supposedly symbolizing a kindled flame of passion—is the 10-billion-yen ($73.8 million) creation of French architect Philippe Starck. Asahi, Japan's second-largest beer maker, built the golden flame to mark its 100th anniversary. "We wanted a building that people would find interesting 30 years from now," says Mr. Takeda.

The blob—or flame, rather—is one of about 60 wacky structures recently built or now going up in Japan that were designed by foreign architects. More than 40 foreign architects have flocked to Japan in recent years, working on projects valued at a total of at least 60 billion yen, industry observers estimate, and many more are on the drawing boards.

Financing the boom are cash-rich Japanese manufacturers, property developers and restaurant owners striving to boost their images by replacing tattered buildings with eye-catching modern constructions. And just as Japanese consumers are turning to prestigious foreign designers for fashion, many companies are paying U.S. and European architects to dress up their buildings with flair.

"There's a belief that if it's the best, it's got to be foreign," says Philip Stewart, an international business manager for PAE International, an American architecture concern that has worked in Japan for more than 30 years. The yen's strength against the dollar is also making foreign names more affordable.

Trend seekers love the new creations. Rows of young Japanese waited for hours in the snow last year when Asahi's French restaurant opened inside the building that supports the golden blob. Its popularity persists: Couples continue to pour in to drink Asahi beer with fine French cuisine, as well as to marvel at twisted green pillars in the halls and silver etchings in the bathrooms, also designed by Mr. Starck.

Japan's obsession with these strange designs is a major change from its traditional approach to architecture, which focused entirely on a building's functions and gave little attention to individual names and styles. Japanese architects often garnered more praise abroad than at home.

Now, in a country with few legal restraints on a building's outward appearance—so long as it can withstand earthquakes—demand for bizarre buildings is surging. In a Tokyo area dominated by shabby concrete houses decorated only with laundry strung from windows, residents find themselves with a new neighbor: a glittering eight-story building by American architect Peter Eisenman. The mirrored facade of the building, which is a showroom for lamps, is covered with an asymmetrical pink-and-blue patchwork pattern.

In a southern suburb of Tokyo, a five-story triangular marble structure that houses an art museum replaced a thatched-roof house; it sits squeezed between an old bakery and the local cemetery.

As much as a fifth of Tokyo is rebuilt every five years, developers estimate, with newer structures competing to stand out more than the buildings built before them. Especially in

Tokyo, "the city itself is organized chaos, which [gives] the architects freedom to express themselves any way they want," says Shi Yu Chen, who has been bringing in foreign architects to "stimulate" Japanese neighborhoods. With so many novel buildings sprouting, says Mr. Chen, the country has "become a theater for international architects."

Larger Projects

That means that even such radical architects as Britain's Nigel Coates often work on larger projects in Japan than they do at home. "There's a greater need in Japan for a status attached to an architectural designer," says Mr. Coates, who says half of his projects are in Japan. "For architects like us that are more avant garde," he adds, "it's very important that we're given an opportunity to realize our potential to the full extent." Japan is where that is most possible, he says.

Five years ago, Mr. Chen spotted some of the creations of Mr. Coates, then an architecture professor little known outside Britain, in a boys' fashion magazine. Since then, Mr. Coates's landmarks around Japan have spread his name worldwide. Among his major works is a 23-meter-tall building in central Tokyo that houses a bar and disco and whose facade resembles a solid brick wall with windows only on the top floor. In the middle of a northern Japanese city, he built a giant Noah's Ark with a Chinese restaurant inside, causing quite a stir among local children.

"In Europe, we are restricted by what the rest of the city looks like," says Mr. Coates. "It will be difficult to build an enormous concrete rock building like Noah's Ark in London."

The splashy buildings, however, are too much for some. Italian architect Aldo Rossi's striking, windowless red-stone hotel in the southern city of Fukuoka is covered with a crisscross of red pillars and horizontal green-metal bars. But set amid blinding neon signs in a seedy part of town, the classical eight-story creation looks rather miserable, says Yoshiyuki Kitamura, a 43-year-old Fukuoka architect.

"If that was built in Italy, it would be a different story," says Mr. Kitamura, who says he generally has great respect for Mr. Rossi's work. "Here, it looks as though it can't communicate in a foreign country."

Architects on the cutting edge are expanding into interior decoration, too. Jasmac Co., a Tokyo-based developer, took the bold step of assigning the interior decoration of a bar and restaurant to Zaha Hadid, an Iraqi-born London architect famous for designing buildings considered too progressive to be built. Striving to satisfy the "ice" theme of the building, Ms. Hadid designed glass dining tables with corners so sharp that managers worried that customers would cut themselves. The glass staircase was so user-unfriendly, says Seiichi Kaga, manager of the building, that a customer once fell and put a hole through the floor. Still, says Mr. Kaga, young Japanese have been crowding the restaurant since it opened in July, and he aims to reach monthly sales of 50 million yen this year.

To be sure, most architects flocking to Japan do only the designing, leaving the nitty-gritty details to Japanese contractors. They pocket as commissions less than 10% of the total budget. Most large-scale public works are still handed to such Japanese architectural powers as Kenzo Tange, who has longstanding relationships with Japanese companies.

Still, skilled foreign architects are gradually grabbing a share of the bigger projects, too, although they charge higher fees. Rafael Vinoly, an Argentine-born American designer, last year obtained a Japanese government contract to build a 130-million-yen conference hall in central Tokyo that will take the form of an ellipse made of glass, resembling the bottom of a ship. Italian architect Renzo Piano is designing the

130-billion-yen terminal for the Kansai International Airport; it will resemble a bird with its wings spread.

Taller Than Mount Fuji

The emergence of foreign architects in Japan is encouraging some Japanese to take a more creative approach to design. And not to be outdone, Japanese construction companies are touting their ability to erect 200-story apartment buildings and structures taller than Mount Fuji.

The rush by Japanese companies to hook up with foreign designers is making some Japanese architects uneasy. Although Kiyokazu Arai, a Tokyo-based architect, certainly feels stimulated by foreigners' novel designs, some companies "don't mind who they get as long as they're foreign and well known," he says.

Some designers question how long Japan's appetite for odd buildings will last. "I wonder if people will keep wanting to be stimulated," says Ittaku Katsuki, chief producer at Creative Box Inc., a Tokyo design company. Eventually, he says, "the buildings will also grow up."

— YUMIKO ONO

December 27, 1990

* * *

Foreigners Get Into Hot Water in Japan's Public-Bath Houses

> *EDITOR'S NOTE: When foreigner meets Japanese in a Japanese public-bath house, there is little chance for* hadaka no tsukiai, *camaraderie in*

nakedness. "Living Japanese Style," a 1989 guide to Japan published by Japan Travel Bureau Inc., advises that the foreigner who doesn't visit a public bath at least once "cannot be said to know Japan." But as our next story relates, too many foreign visits can lay bare the naked truths of culture clash. The Japanese reaction to the flood of foreigners, especially Asian foreigners, visiting their baths in recent years was not particularly edifying. But for evidence that nativism is not a Japanese monopoly, be sure to read this story's surprise ending.

KOFU CITY—Like many older Japanese, 60-year-old Nobuyoshi Takahashi likes nothing better than a relaxing dip in a piping-hot public bath.

The baths were a hit, drawing as many as 300 locals a day. Then the foreigners came.

So five years ago, Mr. Takahashi spent nearly $3 million to build the Ikari Onsen bath house next to his sushi restaurant here, two hours west of Tokyo. He lined his men's and women's tubs with greenish-gray stone for a natural feel and pumps in hot-spring water. The baths were a hit, drawing as many as 300 locals a day.

Then the foreigners came.

"At the peak, there were 40 or 50 of them a day," says Mr. Takahashi, his cheeks flushing with anger. Many hopped in the bath without washing first, a big no-no. A few trimmed their body hair—and left the clippings by the tub. "One time three women were lying on the floor by the tub, smoking cigarettes!" Mr. Takahashi says. "They just laughed and looked away, as if I wasn't there. I couldn't take it—I kicked them." Most of his Japanese regulars stopped coming, so Mr. Takahashi barred all foreigners. "Even a dummy can understand that," he says.

Mr. Takahashi's response was extreme, and local officials later forced him to remove his "No Foreigners" sign. Still, many other public-bath owners tell their own tales of barbaric bathers. Japan's local bath, *sento,* literally money for hot water, has been an institution for 400 years. For many, it's an oasis of serenity away from cramped homes and long commutes. For others, it's a necessity: Many apartments don't have baths, and the sento costs only $2.70 a soak.

Japan's booming population of low-paid foreign laborers—especially Thais, Filipinos, Chinese and Iranians—has discovered the communal tub, and some newcomers are unwittingly violating time-honored bathing rituals. To educate them, Tokyo's sento association has tacked up an eight-language poster illustrating the basics: Soap up and rinse off before easing into the pool, don't waste water and don't get in the tub with your underwear on.

At the Tenjinyu bath house in Tokyo, Kikue Tsutsui sits at the *bandai,* an elevated desk at the entrance of the sento from which she watches bathers on both sides of the wall separating the men's and women's areas. From her perch, she keeps an eye out for rule breakers as three men lounge neck-deep in the tub, which holds as many as 12 people. Mrs. Tsutsui says a dozen or so of her 350 daily customers are foreigners, mostly Asians. Their most common flub: undies in the tub.

"That happens a lot," she chuckles.

Foreigners, most of whom avoid bath blunders, may be getting a bum rap. "You don't want to cause trouble for the people around you, and you don't want to be looked at funny," says Gao Chong Guo, a Chinese studying forestry management in Tokyo. His secret: "I imitate the way of bathing the Japanese use."

But doing as the Romans do can also get you in hot water. Some Japanese break their own rules by taking dips without washing first. Others take towels in the tub, also taboo.

Historically Squeamish

So why do the Japanese get steamed when foreigners transgress? Japan has been squeamish about foreigners' hygiene since opening to commerce in the late 19th century, and locals often resent foreign intrusion into their more intimate gathering places. While Japanese bathers don't seem to mind Caucasian visitors much, says Masako Tanaka, who runs the Takenoyu sento in Kofu City, "The problem is that people dislike those with dark skin."

After local media reported last year that a foreign woman in the area had AIDS, a female Japanese customer gave Ms. Tanaka an ultimatum: Bar the Southeast Asian bathers or she and her friends would stop coming. Ms. Tanaka refused.

"Sento are for people who don't have baths," says Ms. Tanaka, between sips of coffee made with the hot-spring water that feeds her tubs. Ms. Tanaka's big headache is an Israeli who wears her underwear into the water and then launders them by the tub. "You can't keep them out just because they're foreigners. Kicking them out is easy. Coping is hard," she says. "But that's our duty as a public-bath house."

Besides, sento owners have a deeper problem: draining revenues. Kenji Zenimoto, 45-year-old owner of the Honenyu bath house in Tokyo, says his sento once got 500 customers a day, but now serves just 200, about half of them foreigners. The culprit: modern plumbing. "After the [Second World] War, not even a tenth of Japanese homes had baths," says Mr. Zenimoto. "Now, just a tenth don't have them. Sento are finished."

While outdoor hot-spring resorts are more popular than ever among vacationers, neighborhood sento have dwindled in number to 9,100 from 9,700 last year and 23,000 in 1964.

Sharing His Oasis

The decline of the community tub leaves a gap in Japanese life, says Katsuhiko Yamamoto, an insurance executive who often spends weekends sento-hopping. "In the old days, sento served as a social communication center where people exchanged information," he says. The Japanese even have a phrase for the intimacy inspired by communal bathing: *hadaka no tsukiai,* camaraderie in nakedness. "But today, even the young people who go, don't go to communicate," says Mr. Yamamoto. With the decline of sento, "people have no contact with their locality."

Many die-hard sento devotees are people like Minoru Nishimoto, a 68-year-old owner of a Tokyo handbag shop, who for 20 years has dipped daily at Honenyu, despite having a tub at home. "The sento is spacious. It's a great feeling," he says.

Though Mr. Nishimoto says some Honenyu regulars complain about the foreign prostitutes who use the baths, he doesn't mind sharing his oasis with aliens. "I'm used to seeing foreigners," he says, shaving a swath of facial stubble. "And most everyone obeys the rules."

Still, Mr. Nishimoto, who has visited the U.S., doesn't think foreign bathers can achieve true hadaka no tsukiai with Japanese. "No," he says, "the way of thinking is different. Even among Christians, there are Catholics and Protestants who hate one another."

A few nights later, Iranian carpenter Salman Ahmadi and two compatriots visit Honenyu after work. Shy about disrobing, the young men horse around in the dressing room, snatching at each other's underwear. In the bathing area, though, they are all business. Mr. Ahmadi, a burly former weight lifter who has been in Japan for about two years, seems to have the routine down pat. He lathers up from neck to toe, scrubs himself with a towel and rinses away the suds. Then he gets up to leave.

"I don't go in" the tub, Mr. Ahmadi grimaces, pretending to scratch his ribs. "The Japanese, they all have disease."

— MICHAEL WILLIAMS

December 4, 1994

* * *

Japanese Find Moored QE2 a Moving Experience

> *EDITOR'S NOTE: The great luxury ocean liners of the Cunard Line are the stuff of dreams for people around the world. So perhaps it shouldn't have been surprising that when the Queen Elizabeth 2 pulled into the port of Yokohama for 65 days in 1989, hundreds of thousands of Japanese would pay large sums to spend a few hours on board. What is surprising is how some of them spent those few hours. For an eye-opening look, read on.*

YOKOHAMA—In 20 years of sailing the high seas, the Queen Elizabeth 2 has always been synonymous with pricey travel. Now the cash-rich but cautious Japanese are spending millions of dollars for a few hours on the ship—and it never even leaves port.

They get the feel of a luxury ocean liner without the sea-sickness. "They don't care about the view and things like that," says Takashi Shinagawa, a spokesman for Port Yokohama 130 Co., the consortium that chartered the majestic ship to help celebrate the 130th anniversary of the opening of the port of Yokohama. "It's enough for them just to have been on."

> *"They don't care about the view and things like that. It's enough for them just to have been on."*

At a charter fee rumored to total nearly $50 million, it's also a good deal for the QE2's owner, Cunard Line Ltd. As for Port Yokohama 130, it is offsetting much of the 65-day charter cost by selling time on the QE2. For 13,000 yen to 15,000 yen, some 1,200 people a day are buying a three-hour lunch-and-shopping tour. For a mere 50,000 yen to 380,000 yen, an average 700 people a night are staying over.

It doesn't matter that the cheapest room has no window or that the private verandas of the ship's best suites offer a view of tugboats plying the port's murky waters. There is still plenty of Western opulence without ocean turbulence. The Queen Elizabeth Suite features marble bathrooms with gold-plated fixtures. Even the smaller rooms have televisions that pick up on-ship transmissions of such purely foreign fare as a taped concert by Mr. Ostentation himself, the late Liberace.

"One of the most important things of this charter to the Japanese people is that we're showing to them a little bit of the Western world," says Capt. Robin Woodall. "I like to think it's a very good slice of the Western world."

It's also a very photogenic slice, whetting the Japanese appetite for snapshot mementos. The picture-taking starts before boarding, when a professional photographer captures each guest on the gangway for 1,000 yen. The amateur shutterbugs keep the action going throughout the day and everywhere. A young man peers in through a window at the dark green emptiness of the card room and snaps a shot.

Two ladies in flowered silk dresses, freshening up in the public restroom before dinner, decide they just have to record the memory. "Take me here," gushes one, posing between the sink and a still life of flowers. "Here, so the mirror will show behind me."

If the cameras fall silent, it's mainly because the cash registers have taken over. The QE2's 11 boutiques have increased their staff from the usual 21 to 112, and they stay open until midnight to handle all the trade.

Everything from key chains to jewels is selling. Two hundred large white stuffed bears with black-button noses and bright-blue QE2 T-shirts sold out the first day at 6,300 yen each. The outlet for H. Stern jewelers of New York is having trouble keeping its 480,000-yen sapphire-gold-and-diamond watches in stock. And shop manager John Taylor had to place an emergency order for an air-freight delivery of shell-shaped Swiss chocolates—nearly 1.5 metric tons of them.

The hottest sellers are high-priced knickknacks with the QE2 logo that prove the buyer was there, and clothing that's a bargain compared with Tokyo prices. Take a European silk scarf, which normally costs $125 in London and is sold for $190 on the QE2 in Yokohama. That's about a 50% markup, but it's still well under the $315 it would cost in a Tokyo department store.

Meanwhile, clear-cut overpricing doesn't deter the dedicated memorabilia buyer. Here's an elderly couple, emerging from the Harrods outlet: "Look at this, grandma, it cost me 1,300 yen," laughs the grandfather, showing her two postcards and a bookmark. "Just for this."

Many overnight guests, shopaholics or not, find there isn't time for everything. Between the all-included two meals, tea service, rum cocktail, evening show, gambling, disco and midnight buffet, such offerings as the library or the Golden Door health spa fall off the must-do list. "They come in, pick up a dumbbell, try to get on and off the treadmill and they're out in five minutes," says Darryll Leiman, director of the QE2's spa. "They like to take pictures with the tall blond instructor."

Some Unusual Services

The QE2 also offers some unusual services while it's in port. For example, it will have held 13 Western-style weddings before it leaves for Hawaii on Sunday. At a minimum charge of 53,000 yen a head, the package includes pink champagne, lunch and the captain's services as official witness.

The romantic event unfolds with naval precision. "The captain's speeches start at 10:30 a.m., they marry at 10 minutes of 11:00, go to the Grand Lounge where the orchestra is ready to play, and then the bride and groom come down from the balcony," says John Waldron, the ship's cruise director. "On the second dance, the bride often wishes to dance with the captain."

Cross-cultural confusion is mostly avoided thanks to ubiquitous but discreet bilingual employees of Port Yokohama 130. Many of the visitors come from the hinterland. About 60% come courtesy of Japanese corporations, which buy tickets in blocks and offer them as gifts to clients or incentives to employees.

Aiming for Long-Term Gains

Port Yokohama 130 spokesmen say the consortium may only break even on the venture because they aren't selling as many overnight tickets as they had hoped. But the consortium members aren't too worried because, in typical Japanese fashion, they have their sights set on long-term gains. One of the members, Seiyo Corp., the resort-development arm of the Seibu/Saison Group, wants to learn how Westerners run top-class hotels. The other corporate member, Mitsui & Co., has started running cruises around Japan and is picking up tips from the QE2.

The experience is also good for Cunard. Besides the charter fee, which company officials won't disclose, the QE2's owner draws a cut from the boutique sales and all the alcoholic drinks charges from an average of 2,000 customers a day.

Meanwhile, the ship is learning more about how to be an in-port hotel. Before Yokohama, its only previous experience was a 10-day stint for Digital Equipment Corp. in Boston. Now it's scheduled for a six-month Japanese charter starting in December, three months of which will be in the port of Osaka.

Still, the QE2 might do well to weigh anchor as often as possible. Some of its Western clientele have complained that the in-port charters are cutting into the liner's conventional cruising. And there are even a few Japanese who see something amiss in a ship that doesn't move.

"I don't know," says Masako Yoshida, a Tokyo artist. "Somehow to me the QE2 means a ship sailing on the grand open sea. When it's stuck in the dock without moving, it just isn't the QE2."

— ELISABETH RUBINFIEN

June 2, 1989

* * *

For This Reporter, Urban Isn't Just a Way of Life

EDITOR'S NOTE: Unlike the keepers of the French language, who are horrified at the thought of wishing someone a bon weekend, *the Japanese have a seemingly insatiable appetite for foreign words. Take the Japanese word for a man's suit,* sebiro. *It's pronounced seh-bee-roe and it's written in* katakana, *a phonetic script often used for rendering foreign words in Japanese. That's because the word entered the Japanese language a century or so ago as the Japanization of an English word, Savile Row, the London tailoring district. And in a similar vein, after reading the following story you may wish to refer to the author as* Aaah-bahn.

TOKYO—Finally, a country where people really understand the importance of being Urban.

The Japanese have decided that the English word "urban" has a nice ring to it, just as my mother did 43 years ago. I first noticed the trend a few months ago in Nagoya, when I boarded a train that, on close inspection of my paper coffee cup, turned out to be called the Urban Liner. Aside from musing momentarily on what a headline writer might make of the situation ("Urban Lehner Rides Urban Liner"), I gave the matter little thought. But soon I began to discover myself everywhere.

Here was Urban Wide 400 (a new Hitachi refrigerator) and New Era Air Conditioner Urban (Matsushita). There was Natural Urban Cosmetics, men's suits by D'Urban and buildings called Urbannet and Urban Court Moto Azabu and Urban Cloud 8. Cars have such names as Urban Break (Mazda).

Toyota Motor Corp. even named one floor of a Tokyo show-room "Intelligent Urban Life," which some consider a contradiction in terms.

> ## *In Japan, "Urban has become a very general word used for everything."*

Soon it became clear that one of those inexplicable Japanese fads was building up around me, or at least my name. "Urban has become a very general word used for everything," confirms Kim Kawamura of ODS Corp., a Tokyo-based concern specializing in corporate and brand images.

In English, the word urban, which derives from a Latin word meaning city, appears frequently in negative contexts, like "urban blight" and "urban sprawl." Certainly the word has had some negative implications for me. My father, also an Urban, wanted to spare me the name, but my mother insisted that the only thing better than one Urban was two.

In first grade, the class bully took a dislike to the name, which gave me my first opportunity to engage in hand-to-hand combat. My high-school Latin teacher, Sister Peter Verona, referred to me constantly as Urbibus (the ablative plural of my name's Latin root, if I recall correctly). As an adult, I've come to appreciate the name, though I know when I introduce myself on the telephone I'm doomed to be Irvin or Irwin unless I specify: "That's U-R-B-A-N, as in renewal."

By contrast, the Japanese treat urban (and Urban, for that matter) with the utmost urbanity. Linguistically, urban is no odder to them than any other non-Japanese name. Conceptually, *tokai-teki,* the literal Japanese translation of urban, has overwhelmingly positive connotations.

"It suggests the cosmopolitan side of big-city life," says

Kazuhiro Mawatari, a "corporate identity" expert at Tokyo-based Dentsu Inc., the world's largest advertising agency. "In our life style, *inaka,* rural, is bad."

To many foreigners, the notion that Japanese love big-city life seems peculiar: The Tokyo-Yokohama metropolitan area, with its 32 million people, evokes images of rabbit-hutch housing and packed commuter trains.

But let me assure you: If you have to be an Urban, this is the place. To the Japanese, "urban" is the Tokyo that is clean and safe and crisscrossed by trains that run on time; the Tokyo that caters to every taste, from Parisian bistros to smoky Korean barbecue places, from modern jazz hangouts to live sex shows.

"I'm from Tokyo," says Dentsu's Mr. Mawatari. "I think it's very hard to live in. The trains are crowded. The houses are small. But it has so much charm. It has so many faces."

But why use "urban"? Why don't the Japanese just say tokai-teki?

Actually, for most of recorded history they did. Even 14 years ago, when Osamu Yakou bought Urban, a coffee shop under a railway overpass near Tokyo's Kanda Station, tokai-teki was the norm. But Mr. Yakou liked the English name that came with the Japanese shop because it sounded cosmopolitan. Just as Americans will drop a French word to show off their *savoir-faire*, the Japanese drop English words as proof of their sophistication.

("Japanese English," or "Japlish," has its amusing moments. My personal favorite is a chain of coffee shops called, in English, Sports House Italian Tomato.)

Trouble was, when Mr. Yakou bought his coffee shop, "urban" wasn't well understood by Japanese coffee drinkers. Worse, Mr. Yakou relates, they had a hard time remembering the name because they couldn't pronounce it; in Japanese, the *r* sound never follows a vowel in the same syllable.

The solution was obvious and typically Japanese. Mr. Yakou kept the name, which is still written in roman letters on the shop and in red letters sewn on his white work-shirt. But his business card is in Japanese, with "urban" written in a syllabic Japanese script used for rendering foreign words. The effect is to change the pronunciation.

"It's not Urban," sniffs Dentsu's Mr. Mawatari. "It's *Aaah-bahn.*" In Japanese, aaah-bahn is stunningly mellifluous.

Of course, creative uses of "urban" aren't exclusively Japanese. On a recent trip to the U.S., I counted 130 listings in the Manhattan white pages under Urban, including some intriguing ones, such as Urban Bush Women and Urban Truffles Inc.

But to my knowledge, no one in the U.S. has named a product Urban Toilet, nor do American newspapers carry ads headlined "Urbest Mansion Hot News." (Urban, Urbetter, Urbest?)

They do in Japan. There also are shoes touted as Urban Epicurean, cars hawked under advertising slogans such as Urban Dry Stanza (Nissan), buildings called Urban Elegance, and real-estate complexes described as Nice Urban. (We Urbans especially appreciate the latter two sentiments).

Then there is Urb magazine, a bilingual Tokyo magazine for Urbies that recruits staffers (some of whom are called Urb-mates) with the ringing slogan: "Urb Wants You!"

Urbie was a childhood nickname I'd like to forget. But to Kazuhiko Nishi, a computer-software mogul and Urb's publisher, an Urbie, or "Urb-type person," is a thing of mystery, someone who is "hard to define . . . different."

How different? Well, for one thing, an Urbie "doesn't read ordinary magazines," the publisher says. Mr. Nishi, who claims to read hundreds of magazines, isn't an Urbie. "I have more sophisticated taste," he says. But he is convinced that

Tokyo is brimming with unworldly Urb-types, and he has big ambitions for Urb magazine.

Right now, Urb is an eight-page freebie handed out in coffee shops in Tokyo's Minato Ward, with an editorial content that veers between being an about-Tokyo guide and a classified advertising bulletin board, in which Urb-type people offer to teach each other languages or rent each other rooms.

To expand into more wards, Mr. Nishi admits that Urb needs a sharper editorial focus. But the fuzziness of the current concepts is one reason Urb is an Urb and not an Urban.

"Urban is too specific," Mr. Nishi explains. "Urb is more abstract. We'd like to start adding meaning to it."

Actually, a starting point in the search for meaning is at hand. The magazine now offers Urb jackets and Urb T-shirts. Printed on the T-shirt is the Urb philosophy:

> Look lively! Everyone's watching and you're the star.
> The show is called life so be who you want to be.
> A Worker, a poet, a friend. You rule your destiny.
> Choose your part and play it well.
> Work together! You are not alone in a city of millions.
> There is no urb like Tokyo.

— URBAN C. LEHNER

December 7, 1990

* * *

Oh, No! People Keep Calling Me to Find Out Whether I'm Yoko

EDITOR'S NOTE: Yoko Ono and John Lennon had perhaps the most famous East-meets-West marriage in history. Staff reporter Yumiko Ono got a rude reminder of Yoko's fame when she was transferred to New York after four years in The Asian Wall Street Journal's Tokyo bureau. Ms. Ono, incidentally, is not the first Japanese to become a Journal staff reporter; Masayoshi Kanabayashi, who joined the staff in 1976, claims that distinction. Mr. Kanabayashi still reports for the paper from Tokyo. The eight-reporter bureau includes another Japanese national, Norihiko Shirouzu.

NEW YORK—This is a typical message that strangers leave on my answering machine: "We love you," whispers a young woman between muffled sobs. "It has to be Yoko Ono."

Yoko Ono? My name is Yumiko Ono. I'm a 27-year-old reporter, and not even distantly related to the 61-year-old widow of the late rocker John Lennon.

Try telling that to the slew of people who call me day and night, hoping—sometimes demanding—to speak to Yoko. Since moving here four months ago, I've received scads of such calls—from pushy fans, merchants hawking Beatles memorabilia and even an amateur impersonator of Sean Lennon, Yoko's 18-year-old son.

The confusion is easily explained. Like many single women, I chose not to disclose my full name in the Manhattan telephone directory, listing myself simply as "Y. Ono." Thus, people ringing up directory assistance looking for Yoko get my number instead. And the calls come from all over the country.

When Julie Ross, a 25-year-old artist in Westerville, Ohio, came across "Y. Ono" in directory assistance, the listing came as a shock. "I just had to make sure it was her," she said. Of course, it wasn't. But Ms. Ross, who wants to give Yoko a charcoal painting she drew of John, consoled herself by saying, "You sound just like her."

Actually, Yoko Ono's celebrity has always shadowed me. More and more, being an Ono became an onus.

Many fans sound quite earnest when calling. Jamaliya Colbine, a 10-year-old from Bloomington, Indiana, was very apologetic for waking me one recent night. She insisted that she and a friend, Kerstin Picht, also 10, were serious Yoko admirers who "cry sometimes when we think about the unfortunate thing that happened"—John Lennon's 1980 assassination. But when Miss Picht got on the phone, any seriousness evaporated. "I was going to ask for Paul McCartney's number," she said. "He is very cute."

Others offer more creative reasons. Angelica King, a 15-year-old from West Palm Beach, Florida, called to recruit Yoko for a role in a movie she said her father was producing. In fact, her father, Lee King, is a fledgling screenwriter who is working on a script involving the Beatles. But, in a later conversation, he said he never told his daughter, a fanatic Beatles fan, to call. Still, Mr. King allowed that he wouldn't mind having Yoko in his movie if it's ever made, and couldn't resist wondering: "By the way, are you related to Yoko?"

Actually, Yoko Ono's celebrity has always shadowed me. When I was growing up in Queens, New York, classmates kept asking if we were related. "Do you know what would happen if your name were Yoko?" they pestered, as though I'd never made the connection before.

But more and more, being an Ono became an onus. As Yoko began making public appearances this spring to promote her musical, "New York Rock," calls came in from Michigan, Florida and Maine. The NBC television network also gave people ideas, when a character in its sitcom "Mad About You" tried to reach Yoko and joked about looking her up in the phone book. I got five calls that night.

Ono, translated literally as "Little Field," is actually the 54th most-common family name in Japan—roughly akin to "Murphy" in the U.S. There are about 280,000 Onos in Japan alone, say experts in onomastics, the study of proper names. There are also at least three dozen Japanese female names beginning with a Y, including Yuko, Yaeko, Yoshiko and Yoriko—as well as the more common Yoko.

But there are only two "Y. Ono" listings in Manhattan directory assistance—both of us reluctant celebrities. The second is Yoshi Ono, a free-lance photographer, who says he has received more than 100 calls for Yoko in the past year—mainly from hustling entrepreneurs trying to cut business deals with her. Others came from women hoping to convince Yoko that her son, Sean, had fathered their children. (Yoko's agent scoffs at such claims.)

Mr. Ono says he fleetingly considered changing his name or getting an unlisted number but admits that he doesn't understand English well enough to be really bothered. "They're part of my life now," he says of the calls.

Yoko herself, who has never been listed in the Manhattan directory, is sympathetic. "I'm so sorry you're having that problem," she said, squeezing my hand after I introduced myself during an intermission at a performance of her musical. Perpetual pestering she gets from fans isn't just limited to phone calls. Several years ago, one man even broke into her New York apartment in the Dakota building while she slept. Her agent explicitly instructs fans to write to Yoko at her New York address. Don't call us, we'll call you, he says.

Of course, Y. Onos aren't the only ones in the spotlight. Fame can just as easily descend upon any ordinary W. Allen, J. Roberts or C. Crawford. But New York psychologist Sally Peterson suggests that Yoko's air of mystery seems to attract an unusual number of interested strangers.

Many Americans simply want to know how she is holding up. After all, the sway she held over John Lennon is legendary. "People are fascinated by her power and devotion," says Ms. Peterson. Besides, Yoko is a survivor: Her music and art are often denigrated by critics; she got the blame for breaking up the Beatles; and her husband was assassinated before her eyes. "She's not a standard celebrity," Ms. Peterson says.

Yoko's fans aren't so ordinary, either. Some try to decipher every word of her song lyrics in search of hidden meanings, says Brian Hendel, the 28-year-old editor of Yoko Only, a Manhattan fan-club magazine. "You either love her or hate her," he says, adding that her biggest fans tend to be obsessed. Mr. Hendel himself admits sheepishly that, as a teenager, he skipped high school to prowl outside the Dakota, and pumped the owner of the local dry cleaners for tidbits of Yoko gossip.

Which makes me decide that I want to take the coward's way out. I'm unlisting my number and removing Yoko from my life. I'm also warning my cousin in Tokyo, who fantasizes about living in Manhattan, that her life here might be a little bizarre. Her name, as it happens, is Yoko Ono.

— YUMIKO ONO

May 27, 1994

Other Titles in the Tuttle Library

MODERN JAPANESE PRINTS POSTCARDS
by Norman and Mary Tolman

JAPAN: The Art of Living Postcards Sets 1 and 2

JAPAN COUNTRY LIVING POSTCARDS: Spirit ·
Tradition · Style

JAPAN: An Invitation Postcards
(Set 1) Beauty and Splendor, (Set 2) Culture and Tradition

KARHU'S CLASSIC KYOTO POSTCARDS
by Clifton Karhu

BEAUTIFUL JAPAN: A SOUVENIR *photographed by
Narumi Yasuda*

THE BOOK OF TEA *by Kakuzo Okakura*

ZEN FLOWERS: Chabana for the Tea Ceremony
by Henry Mittwer

DOWN THE EMPEROR'S ROAD WITH HIROSHIGE
Edited by Reiko Chiba

HIROSHIGE'S TOKAIDO IN PRINTS AND POETRY
Edited by Reiko Chiba

PAINTED FANS OF JAPAN: Fifteen Noh Drama
Masterpieces *by Reiko Chiba*

SESSHU'S LONG SCROLL: A Zen Landscape Journey
Introduction and notes by Reiko Chiba

THE SEVEN LUCKY GODS *by Reiko Chiba*

INRO AND OTHER MINIATURE FORMS OF
JAPANESE LACQUER ART *by Melvin and Betty Jahss*

NETSUKE: Japanese Life and Legend in Miniature
by Edwin C. Symmes, Jr.

THE WONDERFUL WORLD OF NETSUKE: With One
Hundred Masterpieces of Miniature Sculpture in Color
by Raymond Bushell